MW01616436

I am very pleased to share with you my insights on how boomers will be redefining retirement and shaping the future. This large demographic segment will have a dramatic impact in the years to come. As an investor, boomer, or just an interested observer, you may have also wondered about what the future has in store for you. I hope that this book provides you with a glimpse of what's to come and helps you prepare.

Sherry Cooper
Executive Vice-President, Global Economic Strategist,
BMO Financial Group

Also by Sherry Cooper

The Cooper Files

Ride the Wave

THE NEW
RETIREMENT

HOW IT WILL CHANGE OUR FUTURE

SHERRY
COOPER

VIKING
CANADA

VIKING CANADA

Published by the Penguin Group

Penguin Group (Canada), 90 Eglinton Avenue East, Suite 700, Toronto, Ontario, Canada
M4P 2Y3 (a division of Pearson Canada Inc.)

Penguin Group (USA) Inc., 375 Hudson Street, New York, New York 10014, U.S.A.
Penguin Books Ltd, 80 Strand, London WC2R 0RL, England
Penguin Ireland, 25 St Stephen's Green, Dublin 2, Ireland (a division of Penguin Books Ltd)
Penguin Group (Australia), 250 Camberwell Road, Camberwell, Victoria 3124, Australia
(a division of Pearson Australia Group Pty Ltd)
Penguin Books India Pvt Ltd, 11 Community Centre, Panchsheel Park, New Delhi – 110 017,
India
Penguin Group (NZ), 67 Apollo Drive, Rosedale, North Shore 0745, Auckland, New Zealand
(a division of Pearson New Zealand Ltd)
Penguin Books (South Africa) (Pty) Ltd, 24 Sturdee Avenue, Rosebank, Johannesburg 2196,
South Africa

Penguin Books Ltd, Registered Offices: 80 Strand, London WC2R 0RL, England

First published 2008

1 2 3 4 5 6 7 8 9 10   (RRD)

Manufactured in the U.S.A.

Library and Archives Canada Cataloguing in Publication available upon request

ISBN-13: 978-0-670-06855-5
ISBN-10: 0-670-06855-1

Visit the Penguin Group (Canada) website at **www.penguin.ca**

Special and corporate bulk purchase rates available; please see
www.penguin.ca/corporatesales or call 1-800-810-3104, ext. 477 or 474

In memory of my father,
Irwin M. Sussman

Contents

Introduction

The baby boom has had a profound effect in changing societal norms and dominating economic developments and business activity, and nowhere more so than in Canada. While it occurred in other countries as well—most notably in the United States, Australia, and New Zealand—the baby boom in Canada was the largest in the world. Similarly, the decline in birth rates following the boom has been the most dramatic in Canada; these two phenomena—boom followed by bust—have meant that the boomers represent a larger proportion of the population in Canada than in any other country. During every stage of the boomers' lives they have precipitated change, and the arrival of this generation at late middle age and the traditional retirement years portends new and significant economic, political, and social developments.

Boomers can be usefully divided into two age groups: leading-edge boomers born between 1946 and 1954, and the many more late boomers, born between 1955 and 1966 (or 1965 in the United States). As a group, boomers will redefine retirement just as they have redefined middle age. While much is made in the media about the oldest boomers moving into their 60s, this group is a relatively small proportion of the Canadian and U.S. populations. *Most boomers are in their 40s, with another 20 years or so until traditional retirement.* They still have kids to raise, tuition to pay, and debt at a level well above that carried by their parents at the same age, even adjusted for inflation. These 40-somethings have yet to reach their peak earning and wealth-accumulating years. A small percentage of boomers will retire in the next five years, but a far larger number will hit retirement in the 2020s. *The crest of boomer retirement is not until 2025.*

In this book, I examine the Canadian and global economic implications of this aging population and its impact on government policy, business, financial markets, and society. As well, I zero in on the personal impact of aging and the coming reality for boomers and their families. I cover these issues for the United States as well, because of the close links between the U.S. and Canadian economies, the wealth of American demographic and survey data regarding retirement-related issues, and the fact that Canadians get much of their retirement advice and information from the U.S. media. In addition, most Canadian boomers who decide to spend a meaningful portion of their retirement living outside of Canada will likely do so in the United States.

But this is not your typical retirement book; this is not a personal finance book. There are plenty of those already. This book looks at the transition to late life and what it takes to achieve a successful final third of your life. A successful retirement for most people—be it at age 55, 65, or 75—is to be physically and fiscally independent and active with love and purpose in their lives. Boomers are "retiring" retirement as people in our parents' generation knew it. We will not settle for personal diminishment, social isolation, dependency, and inertia. In the new retirement, boomers will remain active in mind and body, and most of us will continue to be productive well into our eighth decade. Our later years will be more youthful and exhilarating than they were for any previous generation, as we are the healthiest and wealthiest generation ever to retire.

In *The New Retirement* I will examine how we can prepare for the last third of our lives to give ourselves the best chance of physical and mental well-being and financial security. We can age successfully—actually *regenerate* rather than *degenerate*. I will describe the key mid-life predictors of a happy, healthy late life. Most of these predictors are under our control—some are behavioural and some are attitudinal. No longer is our genetic make-up or parental social class a sole determinant of our destiny. *There are things we can do today that will increase the likelihood of our aging well,* adding "life to our years," as well as years to our life. There is a rapidly growing body of scientific research that explains the key processes of healthy maturation and a satisfying late life. Success in life varies from person to person, and it is much broader than simply success in work.

The research suggests there are benefits to aging, as stress diminishes and most people re-evaluate what is important in life. The impulse to be ostentatious and competitive typically wanes; the wise ones are more comfortable in their skin than ever before, and there is time to experience the beauty in the world and to nurture younger people and each other. Older brains are better at dealing with complex situations, having the benefit of so much experience. Emotions can be more easily controlled, and the opportunity to feel joy and have peace of mind is greater than at any other time in our lives. Many studies show that people who have aged well wouldn't want to go back to their childhood, teens, young adulthood, or the rat race years of career achievement in their 40s and 50s. Many are quite content to be right where they are in the life cycle. With advances in our knowledge about the aging process, *many experts now believe there is no reason to suffer enormous and prolonged pain, degeneration, and inactivity before death.*

Of course, financial planning remains a key component to successful retirement. I will show how to determine how much money you will need in retirement and what your options are to achieve that level of wealth. It is no longer considered necessary to shift from stocks to bonds as you near retirement, or that you should ever divest yourself of all of your equity holdings. Boomers have, for the most part, been notoriously bad savers; I will show you some ways to fast-track your retirement savings and stretch the value of your retirement nest egg.

Boomers were the "new generation" that transformed societal and cultural norms as well as politics. Boomers are far less traditional and conservative than their parents were. We broke away from what our elders expected of us and challenged their assumptions from across the generation gap. Even as the radicals and free thinkers of the 1960s became the yuppies of the 1980s, boomers continued to set new standards for themselves and their children. Unlike the previous generation, most boomers won't have worked for a single employer for 40 years. Many will have had multiple careers, and most do not have gold-plated, "old-fashioned," defined benefit pension plans that guarantee a level of income for the rest of their lives.

What Will Boomer Retirement Look Like?

The subject of retirement conjures up a variety of thoughts and feelings. Of course it sometimes triggers fears of old age and infirmity, but most people see it as a happy time, a less-stressful time to do things they've always wanted to do—a time for themselves and for family and friends. Nevertheless, for many healthy boomers it will be difficult to adjust to a life without a pre-determined schedule or a defined sense of purpose. Many will miss the trappings of their former jobs—the general buzz of the office, the sense of accomplishment when a project has been done well and in good time, the computer support, and the financial security of a regular paycheque. If you have never fixed your own computer problems or lived without a dental plan, it could be quite an adjustment.

An increasing number of people, therefore, will choose a phased-in retirement, working on a more flexible basis and maintaining a healthy, active lifestyle for well into their seventh and eighth decade. People will view this time as a period of regeneration, and that trend is likely to become more pervasive as the bulk of the boomers move into their 60s.

The aging populations of developed countries will have a significant impact on the economy, markets, and health care. A labour shortage has already begun to emerge as boomers leave the senior ranks of the workforce. This shortage will be especially troublesome in Canada, and government is already responding, introducing policies and pension reforms to encourage boomers to postpone their full retirement from work.

Employers will increasingly entice seasoned boomers to stay on the job to preserve continuity, experience, and customer relationships built over many years. Scores of boomers whose jobs don't require excessive physical exertion will remain on company payrolls full time well beyond traditional retirement age. Many boomers will need to work longer and to save and invest more aggressively to top up their nest eggs. It is serendipitous that businesses and public organizations will offer flex-time, part-time positions, job-sharing, telecommuting, consulting positions, and more to extend the productivity of their older workers. In both Canada and the United States, investments in labour-saving technology, stepped up immigration, and outsourcing will also help to fill the labour gap.

Many boomers will take on new challenges or pursue long-held dreams, remaining engaged and purposeful well beyond age 65. Philanthropy and volunteerism will also blossom as boomers give back to the community and the world. An active, happy Act III will be a hallmark of the new retirement.

Chapter 1

The New Retirement

Canadians have been the world leaders in early retirement. According to a January 2006 global retirement study by the American insurance company AXA, a great majority of Canadians have voluntarily retired before the minimum legal age (Chart 1).[1] This has been especially true in Quebec, where a whopping 92 percent of all retirees left work early. The minimum legal retirement age varies among businesses and governments and often depends on time in service and the type of job. Of the 78 percent of Canadians who retired early, 66 percent did so voluntarily. This is a good deal higher than the voluntary early-retirement ratio of 59 percent in the United States, 38 percent in Germany, and only 16 percent in Japan.

Yet today's pre-retirees in Canada, the boomers, do not view retirement as it was for their parents, the end of their working life. While 58 percent of working boomers surveyed said they would like to work after retirement, among today's retirees only 19 percent of men and 9 percent of women still earn a paycheque (Chart 2). Even with these low percentages, Canadians and Americans are the most likely to hold a paying job in retirement—trailing only the industrious Japanese.

Chart 1

Retiring Prior to Normal Retirement Age
(percent of retired population)

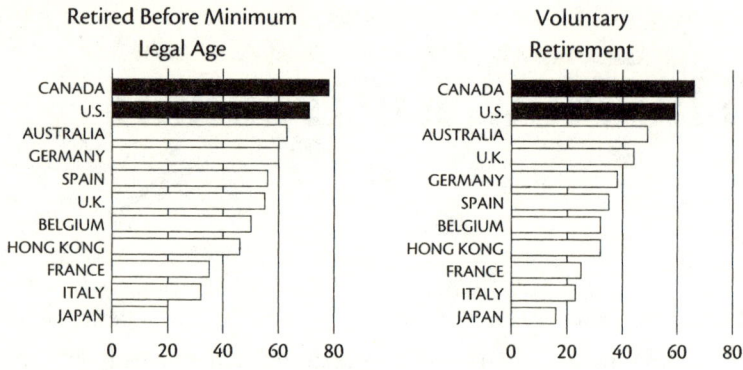

Source: AXA Retirement Scope, Wave 2, 2006.

Chart 2

Planning to Hold a Paid Job after Retirement
(percent)

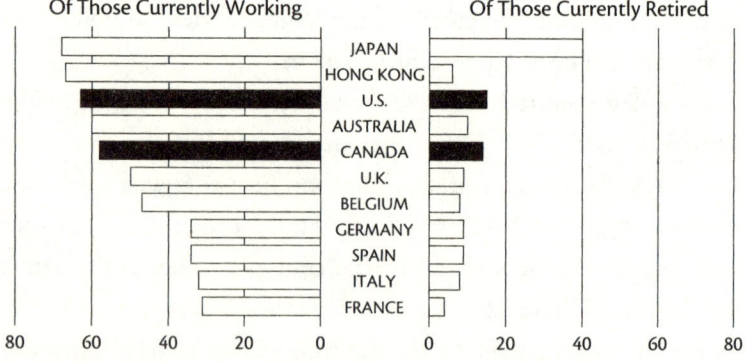

Source: AXA Retirement Scope, Wave 2, 2006.

Chart 3

Raising the Retirement Age?
Limit up to Which Retirement Age Can Be Raised (mean age)

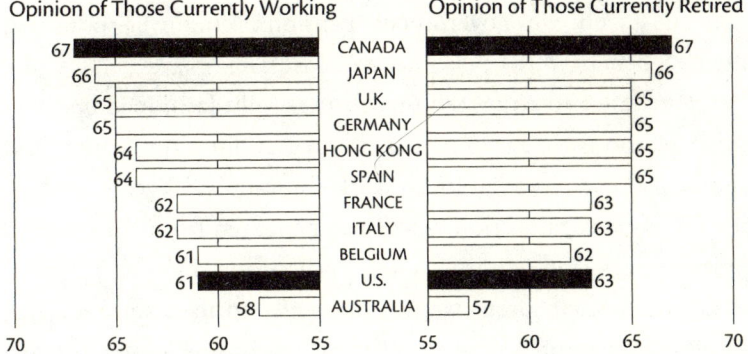

Opinion of Those Currently Working   Opinion of Those Currently Retired

Source: AXA Retirement Scope, Wave 2, 2006.

Interestingly, Canadian responders to the AXA survey are in favour of increasing the minimum retirement age to as high as 67, well above the age limit acceptable in most other countries. In Australia, for example, the maximum acceptable limit was reported as 58, compared to 62 in much of Europe and 65 in Britain (Chart 3).

From a financial point of view, it is retired Canadians of the *boomer-parent* generation who, along with their American counterparts, most typically have a comfortable retirement. An overwhelming majority of Canadian and U.S. retirees surveyed found their standard of living was maintained or improved in retirement. Canadians have retirement income that is the highest in the world after retired Americans, and they consider it to be more than adequate.

Today's retired boomer parents are enjoying the fruits of postwar industrial growth in Canada and the United States. They are a relatively small segment of the population, alive during the Depression and the Second World War. They know how to save, and most rely on government pensions, employer-sponsored defined benefit (DB) pensions and insurance plans. This is the last generation to enjoy the prevalence of old-fashioned employment pensions that promised a lifetime annuity for worker and spouse—the last generation to work commonly 30 years or more for the same organization. They also benefited from the surge in house prices and equity values brought on by the surge in demand as their progeny, the boomers, formed families and exhibited an unprecedented aptitude for consumption. In addition to this bounty, today's retired Canadians are among the healthiest in the world. They like the Canadian health-care system and report that it is as good as, or better than, any in the world—and is at least on par with that of the United States.

Canadian and American boomer workers are the most likely among the countries studied in the AXA survey to expect a comfortable retirement with sufficient funds. Yet only 20 percent of working Canadians responded that they know how much income they will need in retirement. Almost 80 percent of the working Canadians interviewed said they began planning for retirement while still in their 30s. Americans said roughly the same thing. The favoured way to prepare for retirement among Canadians is through RRSPs and life insurance to augment government pension programs—the Canada or Quebec Pension Plans (CPP or QPP). Just over half of working Canadians reported that they set aside money to invest in stocks and bonds; 45 percent contribute voluntarily through their employer; and only 34 percent plan to rely on real estate investments to pay for retirement spending.

Living Longer and More Flexibly

A recent study,[2] commissioned by the Bank of Montreal to understand better the financial needs and concerns of boomers, surveyed 5,325 Canadian financial decision-makers aged 45 and older who had financial assets of at least $25,000. The results suggest that *Canadian boomers will redefine retirement:* for them it will not begin at a fixed point, but over a period of time during which they gradually move from a high-paced lifestyle to a slower, less-pressured pace. Retirement for boomers will be far more active than it has been for earlier generations. Many see retirement as providing an opportunity to pursue new business or community interests, return to school or self educate, travel to new places, and pursue leisure-time activities. Pre-retirees expect to spend less time around the house than previous generations did and spend more time working. They say the primary reason for working is to remain mentally active, to keep in touch with people, and, only thirdly, to earn money.

As a group, boomers will redefine retirement, just as they have been changing societal and cultural norms since they reached pubescence, maybe even before. For example, gender roles are no longer so distinctive. More people live as singles or in same-sex relationships than ever before. Birth rates have fallen, the age at first marriage has risen, and women are having children much later. It is no longer uncommon to hear of women having their first baby in their 40s. Accompanying these trends, not surprisingly, has been a rise in infertility problems and treatment, as women's fertility continues to peak sometime around age 20. As well, more women than ever before have chosen not to have children at all.

The whole concept of family and "normal" lifestyles has shifted. Single-parent households have become more common, as have blended families. Adult children often live at home well into their 20s, as university costs have increased sharply, putting a debt burden on both students and parents. Single-person households are quite common, covering the full spectrum of ages. Indeed, in the most recent census, the traditional family of mom, dad, and the kids was outnumbered by new household forms.

Boomer women fought and won the right to enter professional and academic graduate programs, and many have successfully attained leadership roles in their chosen fields. Women are now heavily involved in what used to be male-dominated fields, and many are the single heads of households or earn significantly more than their partners. They have had many more choices than their moms did, and they have defined their roles as "mother" and "mate" in ways radically unlike those they experienced as children.

This trend has crested, however, as younger boomer and Generation-X mothers have increasingly chosen to be stay-at-

Chart 4

Female Participation Rates Have Peaked

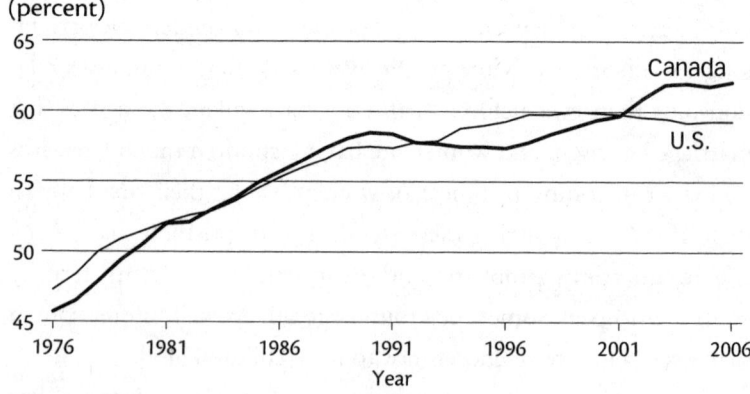

(percent)

Canada: Females, 15+   U.S.: Females, 16+

Sources: Statistics Canada, U.S. Bureau of Labor Statistics.

home moms, at least while their children are very young. The participation rate of women in the workforce peaked in 2004 in Canada and 1999 in the United States (Chart 4). Many now have the opportunity to return to work when their children are older.

A Bureau of Labor Statistics study in the United States compared labour-force participation among mothers of infants by husbands' income level and mothers' education and ethnicity.[3] The biggest declines in workforce participation, as expected, came among mothers with a bachelor's degree or more, followed by women with husbands in the top 20 percent of income earners. But all other demographic categories showed declines too, including women with husbands whose earnings fell into the middle range. The "Mommy-track" trend is most evident among mothers of children under age one. Workforce participation rates of all married mothers of infants fell about 8 percentage points since 1997 to 51 percent in 2004. The decline for mothers of three- to five-year-old children was less than half as large, but workforce participation for them was still down a significant 3.4 percentage points to 63.6 percent.[4]

There are many reasons women leave the labour force when they have a baby: a desire to nurture their children in their first year or so; poor quality and/or the high cost of available child care; lack of extended maternity leave; lack of flexible return-to-work options; and a decision to switch to a more family-friendly career. Canadian women are legally entitled to a full year of maternity leave without jeopardizing their jobs. During that year they are covered by employment insurance. New American moms have always taken shorter maternity or parental leave, mostly without pay, than do their Canadian counterparts.

Divorce rates, which surged in the seventies, peaked in 1987 in Canada and 1981 in the United States, and thereafter the boomers seemed to have settled down (Chart 5). The spike in Canada in 1987 was due to a change in Canadian divorce laws which introduced a no-fault provision, making it easier for many to get divorced. From a financial perspective, virtually nothing can be as damaging to household wealth and a retirement plan than divorce, particularly if it occurs in middle age—late enough in life that asset accumulation has been significant.

These societal changes initiated by the boomer generation inevitably affect retirement. So do medical advances and healthy living, which have both markedly increased longevity. Retirement was never expected to last 20 years or more. Most boomers do not have the financial means to support themselves for decades at their pre-retirement living standard—particularly as the number of people covered by old-fashioned defined benefit pension plans

Chart 5

Divorce Rates Decline

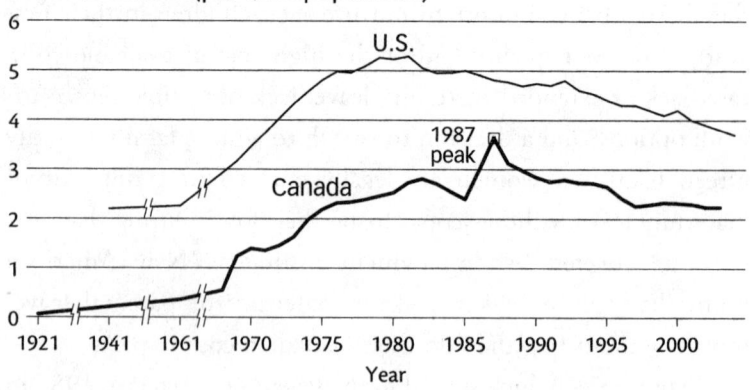

Divorce Rates (per 1,000 population)

Sources: Statistics Canada, U.S. Department of Health and Human Services.

has fallen in recent years. Of the DB plans that still exist, many are less generous than in earlier decades.

Many boomers do not want to be without work for 20 years or more. Although many retire early, especially public sector workers who can qualify for maximum pensions by age 55, an increasing proportion will develop new careers, start new businesses, or engage in meaningful and demanding volunteer work. The boomers are the healthiest and wealthiest generation in history. Most boomer households are accustomed to a regular paycheque; and those with better-than-average incomes cannot live similarly on the Canada Pension Plan, which pays a maximum of less than $11,000 per year in today's dollars.

In addition, boomers are the "sandwich generation," often responsible for the care and support of elderly parents while, at the same time, helping their children pay for their education, early-career expenses, and, ultimately, their first home and their grandchildren's education. This places an enormous burden on boomers' time and finances. Many of these commitments are uncertain and open-ended, and therefore difficult to anticipate and plan for.

So for both want and need, boomers will work longer and more flexibly. Thanks to major technological advances, many boomers can work from home or virtually anywhere else. Businesses will need the talent and experience of boomers and offer phased-in retirements and other enticements to work well beyond traditional minimum retirement age.

As well, as boomers strive for both a healthy and happy retirement and take steps to improve their financial security in the later decades of their lives, they will remain active far longer than their parents did. For many, this will mean working longer, taking on a variety of assignments, and reducing the number of years they operate without a paycheque. They will begin to save in earnest and invest more aggressively than their parents did; bonds will not be their favoured investment vehicle. Boomers will keep the bulk of their retirement savings in the stock market, at least until very late in life. Moreover, financial innovation will continue to generate alternative investment and insurance products to help boomers manage their finances in later life.

With boomers so dominant in the labour force, especially in Canada, the greying of the population will have profound effects on the workforce, the workplace, financial services, and travel and leisure offerings. New styles of living will continue to develop, such as assisted-living facilities with myriad activities, communities of semi-retirees offering fitness and leisure opportunities, and many health-care-centred living arrangements. We have already seen these trends emerge. Travel offerings, book clubs, and discussion groups on virtually any subject are popping up for the older boomers. Bridge lessons are very popular, as are university courses for the mature student. Active minds and active bodies will be the hallmark of the new retirement. It will be more a period of regeneration than a period of degeneration. Boomers will give new meaning to the term "aging well."

KEY POINTS

- Canadians have historically been world leaders in early retirement, voluntarily retiring before the minimum legal retirement age has been reached.

- Today's boomers view retirement differently than their retired parents, and they expect a comfortable retirement with sufficient funds.

- Boomers see retirement as a period of regeneration rather than degeneration.

- Societal norms have changed with the boomers. They have redefined the role of women, created new lifestyles, and challenged the idea of the typical household.

- Labour shortages and rising healthful life expectancy will encourage boomers to work longer, helping to meet the financial demands of this "sandwich generation."

- Flexible work styles and information technology will aid boomers in combining more leisure with continued labour-market participation.

- The achievement of financial security will require many boomers to work longer and to save and invest more aggressively.

- Aging well will be a hallmark of succcessful retirement for boomers.

Chapter 2

The Generational Divide

The characteristics of a particular generation are a reflection of its collective experiences, the ones that shape that generation's values and attitudes—its so-called "markers." They define, unify, and differentiate that generation.[1]

The Boomer Parents, Born 1901 to 1945

The boomer parents can be divided into two groups: those born between 1901 and 1925, the age group that fought the Second World War; and those born between 1926 and 1945, the Depression babies, who were still in their teens or younger during the war. What they share is a core set of very traditional values—discipline, self-denial, hard work, team work, obedience to authority, and financial and social conservatism. In 2005, there were 5.9 million people in the boomer-parent generation in Canada, representing 18 percent of the population. In the United States they amount to about 17 percent of the population.

They came of age expecting clear and distinguishable gender roles. In Canada, they gained from the newly established social welfare system and are the primary beneficiaries of the CPP. In the United States, they have enjoyed a solvent social security and Medicare system that many now believe will collapse under the weight of the aging boomers. Today, they are activist senior citizens with strong and vocal lobbying power. Having endured two world wars, this generation in Canada saw the value of an activist government, but unlike their generation in the United States, they did not see a pro-business government as the ideal model.

The boomer parents were the children of the Depression, when birth rates plunged and the unemployment rate in Canada surged to 27 percent. They knew hardship and self-denial. They graduated from uncrowded schools and universities. They got there first, but missed all the fireworks. Indeed, getting there first was their greatest advantage, allowing them to climb the corporate and political ladders with relative ease. These were the "traditional" folks the boomers rebelled against with alternative lifestyles and women in the workforce (Chart 6).

The Boomers, Born 1946 to 1966 in Canada (1965 in the United States)

The postwar baby boom didn't happen everywhere, only in Canada, the United States, Australia, and New Zealand. War-ravaged Europe and Asia did not see the same phenomenon. The baby-boom countries have a younger population than the rest of the industrial world, a considerable demographic advantage.

The Canadian baby boom was spectacular: it was proportionately the biggest in the world—bigger than the U.S. boom and lasting a year longer. There are 10.1 million boomers in

Chart 6

Profound Demographic Implications

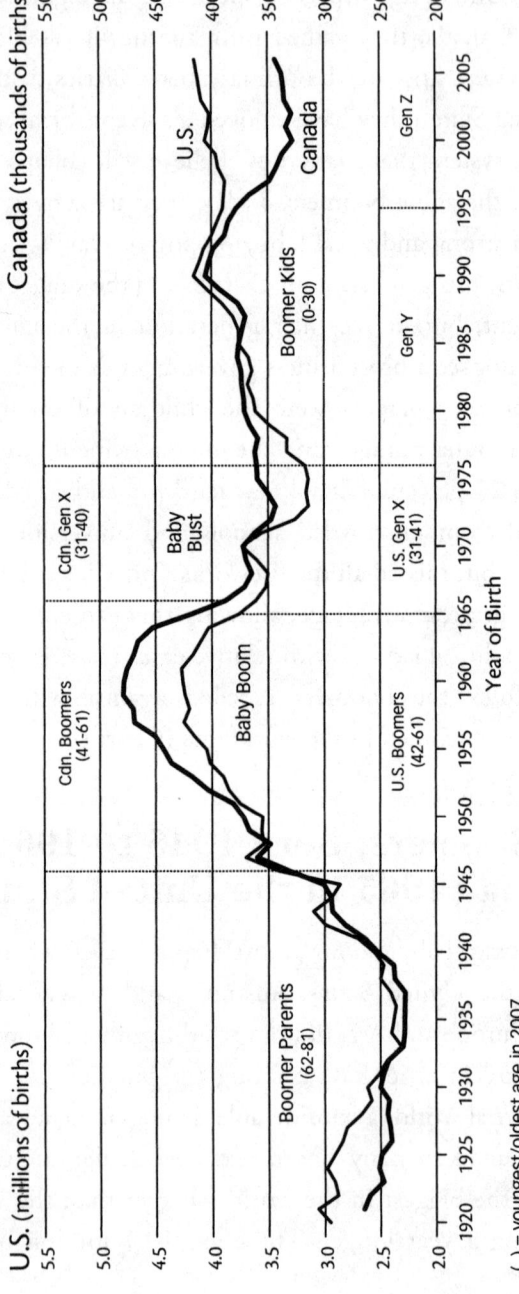

( ) = youngest/oldest age in 2007

Sources: Historical Statistics of Canada, National Center for Health Statistics.

Canada today, representing a whopping 32 percent of the population. This compares to 78 million boomers in the United States, representing 26 percent of the population. After a multidecade rise, the fertility rate in Canada peaked in 1959, at an exceptionally high 3.9 children per woman, before falling sharply during the 1960s. In the United States, fertility rates peaked at 3.7 children per woman in 1957 (Chart 7). In the 1960s, three- and four-children families were relatively common, especially in Canada, but today they are downright rare in both countries.

Economies with rapidly growing populations and labour forces enjoy far stronger growth in consumption and economic activity. Thus the boomers in both Canada and the United States grew up in times of economic bounty. From 1946 to the mid-1970s, economic prosperity and progress were evident everywhere. And

Chart 7

Fertility Rates Stabilizing
Fertility Rates (births per woman of reproductive age)

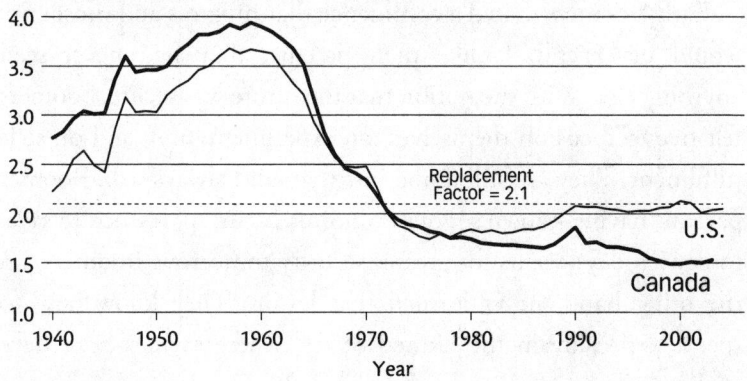

Sources: Historical Statistics of Canada, (U.S.) National Center for Health Statistics.

for a family to live well, only one income was sufficient, whereas two incomes are often required today.

The boom was the result of huge pent-up demand and the postponement of family formation during wartime. With the end of the conflict came an explosion in population growth, a shift from "guns to butter" in the domestic economy, and the mass-market adoption of the automobile. With the family car, and the subsequent two-car family, suburban development skyrocketed. The huge number of young families with children necessitated affordable new homes. With improved transportation, these homes could be built farther from the city centre, and that in turn led to the advent of the shopping centre, the widespread building of suburban schools and other public facilities, the highway system, and a growing consumer market. Consumerism was boosted further by mass-market advertising on the new home-entertainment medium, the television. Boomers are the first generation to have grown up with TV.

Youth was celebrated and the world was good; that is why nostalgia is so big among boomers. And boomers today continue to celebrate youth, refusing to quietly accept the constraints of their own middle age.

Early boomers shared a confidence that progress and prosperity would never end. Unlike their parents, they had never seen anything else. With the notion that the future was secure, boomers felt free to focus on themselves, on experimentation, and on self-fulfilment. They are still doing just that, and always will. Boomer parents, having known serious economic hardship, learned to save, to deny today's wants for greater security tomorrow. Boomers, on the other hand, never learned that lesson. They know how to spend, especially in the United States, where savings rates have traditionally been below levels in Canada. The American boomer is an accumulator par excellence. *Today, savings rates are near record lows in both countries, and the largest share of household net worth is homeowners' equity rather than more-liquid investible financial assets.*

As Canadian household wealth hit record highs thanks to the boom in house prices, we too squirreled away less of our income. Canadian boomers, though not the spendthrifts that Americans are, certainly are more willing to splurge on the extras than their parents were, even if it means going into debt. In the booming cities of western Canada, there are long waiting lists for Porsches, Rolexes, designer handbags, and all the other expensive goodies that affluent American consumers so covet.

The Early Boomers, Born 1946 to 1954

Boomers may be divided into two distinct groups: the early, or leading-edge, boomers and the late boomers. In Canada, the early boomers came of age during the positive atmosphere of the Centennial celebration in 1967, while the late boomers approached maturity in the negative atmosphere in 1970 surrounding the FLQ crisis and the use of the War Measures Act and the Parti Québécois victory in 1976. In the United States, the divide was whether they came of age during the Vietnam War or during the Watergate period.

There are far fewer early boomers than there are late boomers, as fertility rates rose year after year and did not peak until the late 1950s. This was great, by the way, for early-boomer men in the dating and marriage market. Given that men generally marry women their age or younger, as birth rates rose year after year there were many more potential mates for men. Consequently, there are many more unmarried early-boomer women than there are unmarried early-boomer men, and there always will be.

Women learned to fend for themselves, financially and socially. With divorce rates rising, early-boomer wives learned that they could not necessarily rely on their husbands for financial security. This, in combination with the pill and abortions on demand, might help to explain the surge in female boomers in universities, graduate and professional schools, and in the labour force.

In societies where men have many potential mates to choose from, and women have relatively few, the average first-marriage age rises, as men are in no hurry to marry with so many women to choose from. Societal norms for women become more liberal, as more women do not become stay-at-home moms or even moms at all. Compare this to societies where marriageable women are in relatively short supply—think of India, China, and many Muslim countries. There, men, fearing the competition of other men, marry younger to remove their "best option" from the pool of unmarried women. Women are also generally more restricted in their behaviour, as men are more likely to prefer someone who will be content as a stay-at-home mom, and virginity and faithfulness are prized.

The members of the early-boomer cohort have experienced economic good times and want a lifestyle at least as good as the one they had as children during the 1950s. The early boomers in both Canada and the United States got there first. They were the first of their very large generation to enter the schools and universities, the job market, and the housing market, and they will be the first to retire in the coming decade. They were, on average, financially better off than late boomers at the same age. They have outpaced their parents in educational and economic achievement, although much of the economic abundance was the result of two-income families.[2]

The Late Boomers, Born 1955 to 1966 in Canada (1965 in the United States)

Members of the late-boomer cohort in the United States and Canada had a very different experience. Rather than being first in line during the booming fifties, they were last in line during the sixties. They entered elementary schools already crowded by their elders. Their childhood experience, in the United States, of bomb shelters and air-raid drills was daunting, but the real distinguishing factor for this age group came with the trauma of Watergate. The Watergate scandal changed those people coming of age in America by adding to an era of unease, uncertainty, and economic malaise; Canadians, through the wonders of television, could not help but be affected as well. And Canadians had their own problems, with Quebec separatism and western alienation. Over this period as well, oil prices surged with the first OPEC oil crisis in 1973 and inflation and economic stagnation ensued.

While much was made in the media about the oldest boomers turning 60 in 2006, this group is a relatively small proportion of the Canadian and U.S. population. *Most boomers are in their mid-40s, with another 20 years or so to go until retirement.* They still have kids to raise, tuition to pay, and debt at a level well above that carried by their parents at the same age, even adjusted for inflation. They have yet to hit their peak earning and wealth-accumulating years.

A small percentage of boomers will retire in the next five years, but a far larger number won't hit retirement until the 2020s and beyond. *The boomer–retirement wave will not crest until 2025.* Early boomers will get to the financial markets first, before the real onslaught of demand for stocks, bonds, and other investment vehicles. They will benefit from the increasing price of these assets as demand rises, just as they benefited from the increasing price of their homes.

The boomers, the iconic generation of the postwar period, now have greying hair or no hair at all, failing eyesight, and sagging jowls. Even the youngest baby boomers are over 40, and the oldest are now over 60.

This was the first generation to go to university in mass numbers, to postpone parenting until later in life, to make women in the workforce commonplace, along with dual-income families and daycare. Young women began to move into previously male-dominated fields, while marriage rates declined precipitously and cohabitation and divorce rates increased until boomers finally began to settle down.

Boomers have also brought to the mainstream a strong interest in health and fitness. This healthier and highly ambitious generation is less inclined to accept that their extended retirement period must be synonymous with stagnation or even slowing down. For many, the traditional retirement age of 65 will long pass before they feel the need or desire to stop working. Moreover, boomers are the first generation to take advantage of telecommuting and the flexibility provided by technology to work anywhere at any time.

There is no doubt that the demand for "fountain-of-youth" products and services will continue to grow rapidly, boosting the number of cosmetic surgeons, laser eye centres, fitness clubs, spas, weight-loss clinics, health food stores, preventive medicine and longevity specialists, joint replacements, youth-promising creams and potions, and pharmaceuticals from Botox to Viagra. In recent years, there has been a proliferation of TV ads for menopause and osteoporosis drugs, prostate and erectile dysfunction medication, not to mention financial planning for the coming retirees. These ads were rare in the eighties, when boomers were young and climbing the corporate ladder. But while the boomers struggle to stay young, it may also be true that ageism and age discrimination will diminish as 60-somethings and even 70-somethings keep working and remain active in most aspects of their lives.

Generation X, Born 1966 to 1976

The period just after 1965 is known as the baby bust. Those born during that period—today's 30-something-year-olds and those recently turned 40—have been called Generation X. They are relatively few in number, as fertility rates plunged in those years to a low in 1976 of about 1.8 children per woman in Canada and the United States. In Canada, the decline was particularly pronounced, as it fell from a higher level and has continued to slide pretty much ever since.

Canada consequently faces a more acute labour shortage than does the United States, and thus faces a sharper decline in economic growth unless alternative sources of labour or increased productivity can fill the gap. In general, Canada must do more to keep boomers on the job, encourage immigration, expand outsourcing, and invest in labour-saving technology to improve productivity growth—even more so than will be necessary in the United States.

Generation Xers are next in line for the boomers' jobs, although most boomers still have a way to go before their careers peak. Most of current senior management in business, health care, the professions, and public service are in their mid- to late-50s and will be retiring relatively soon and en masse.[3] A dearth of leadership is on the way, but in many cases the age gap between senior leadership and the next level down is relatively small.

Expect older boomers to remain on the job, at least part time, for longer than their parents, and for 40-something boomers to move up fast. Generation Xers will finally squeeze up, but there are still many ahead of them. Unless they run their own companies, Xers are unlikely to refill the depleting ranks of the Young President's Organization, for under-40-year-old CEOs of meaningfully sized companies.

Generation Xers came into a world far different from the *Leave It to Beaver* existence of the early boomers. For the younger generation, mom was at work, and "mom and dad" often became "mom or dad" as divorce rates surged. These were the original latchkey kids. Raised on *Sesame Street* and MTV, and introduced to computers in high school, they span the beginning of the technology revolution. They remember television before cable, vinyl records, and life before the PC. The defining developments for this generation were the computer and cable television.

Their disappointments were real. Divorce, recession, and economic restructuring, Chernobyl, Tiananmen Square, Meech Lake, and the Challenger disaster were markers for this generation. The early-eighties recession put their parents out of work, and the early-nineties recession, the longest in the Canadian postwar period, ravaged the Gen Xers just as they were starting their careers. Unlike the early boomers, who believed economic prosperity would last forever, Xers are more pragmatic and skeptical.

Even a university degree did not assure them success—for many it guaranteed nothing. They suffered the consequences of education inflation. Today, a bachelor's degree is often required for the most basic entry-level position, and a degree costs far more than it used to. Sharp cutbacks in federal money for universities have increased the cost of tuition, and many Xers were left with crushing school-loan payments, as are their younger cousins today.

This was the first generation to have a lower standard of living than their parents did at the same age. They have been hurt by restructuring, as the last in is often the first to go. The answer for many is their technical expertise. This is their competitive advantage, as they are better-trained technically than the boomers. But the bursting of the tech bubble in 2000 hit them hard. After the surge in demand for their skills to fix the Y2K problem, the Nasdaq crashed, technology workers were laid off, and many former 25-year-old tech millionaires were penniless. Gradually, the demand for tech skills has rebounded, but to nowhere near the level of the past.

Generation Xers postponed marriage and having children, and fertility rates in Canada have plummeted. Unlike the Hispanic influx in the United States, immigrants in Canada haven't had enough children to offset the falling birth rates of native-born Canadians. Thirty-somethings today are very different from the boomers at the same age. They are not compulsive achievers and accumulators; they work to live, not live to work.

Generation Y, Born after 1976[4]

These are mostly the boomers' kids, with some of the younger ones the kids of the Gen Xers. The "echo" baby boom was proportionately much smaller in Canada than it was in the United States, reflective of the greater drop in fertility rates north of the border, especially in Quebec. Canadian fertility rates fell sharply below those in the United States after 1979, and the gap has widened since. The proportional difference is especially large in the under-20 group (Chart 8). There are 10.1 million boomers in Canada (32 percent of the population) and only 8.3 million young people age 20 and under (25.7 percent of the population).

In the United States, in contrast, fertility rates rose since the mid-seventies to their highest level in almost 20 years by 2000, and now average 2.1 children per woman, compared to only 1.5 in Canada. The higher fertility rate of Hispanic women who have entered the United States is partly responsible, but even white native-born American women boast a fertility rate of 1.7. There are now an estimated 78 million boomers in the United States (26 percent of the population), but there are 86.1 million kids under the age of 20, accounting for an even larger 29.1 percent of the total. The cohort of older boomer kids, age 22 to 29, is proportionately similar (10.9 percent of the U.S. population) to that in Canada (11 percent). American kids born since the crossover year in fertility rates, 1979, proportionately far outnumber those born in Canada. The economic advantage of a relatively young and rapidly growing population is meaningful.

Chart 8

Population Share by Age
(percent)

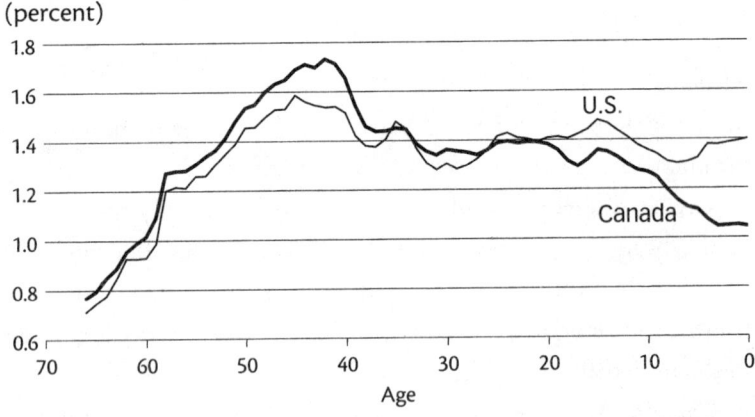

Sources: Statistics Canada, U.S. Census Bureau.

The oldest boomer kids—the most senior of whom will turn 32 in 2008—come from families with the lowest child-to-parent ratio in history. These children frequently arrived to parents who desperately wanted them. The abortion rate peaked in 1980 and has since declined gradually. Infertility treatment has increased sharply in the past 25 years, as many boomer women found they had postponed motherhood too long and sought medical help.

What makes today's U.S. population growth trend different from the surge in the late 1960s is that it is a long, slow, rising wave, and there is likely to be no immediate fall-off. The number of births per year is projected to remain fairly stable at around 4 million, in contrast to the decline after the previous baby boom, when births per year in the early 1970s fell to 3.1 million. Long-range projections by the U.S. Census Bureau indicate that birth rates are expected to rise to 4.3 million in 2010 and 4.6 million in 2020. U.S. fertility rates of 2.1 are roughly the replacement population rate; thus the growth in population in the United States is now driven largely by immigration. This is a reflection of two trends: more children coming into the United States, and immigrants in general having higher fertility rates than that of the native population. (We cannot capture the full effect of immigration in the data because so many are illegal Mexican immigrants who often, but not always, slip undetected through the census surveys.)

There is another key difference from the 1960s boomer-driven population jump: the share of kids in the U.S. population is much smaller today as the country's population rises to over 300 million. Youth comprised 39 percent of the population in 1966, but only 28 percent today. And by 2020 that will dip even further.

Kids today are more colour-blind than ever before and are increasingly becoming citizens of the world. They are more racially and ethnically diverse than their parents' generation, and are therefore more tolerant and accepting of differences.

Boomer kids are divided into "haves" and "have-nots" according to their access to technology and their ability to acquire important technical and traditional reading and math skills early in life. This technology gap—the digital divide—will tend to exacerbate the widening gap between rich and poor children and teens in Canada and, especially, the United States.

These are the children of the computer age, the internet, cable television, cellphones, video games, iPods, free trade, globalization, and multiculturalism. They are the best-travelled, most sophisticated youth in history. Television and videos have expanded their horizons. While many have seen a return to traditional family values, all have been exposed to the realities of life at a very early age. Television tells them everything, and it is augmented by the internet.

They are also the most competitive kids in history. Their standardized testing scores for university are actually going up, even as the lower-level basic-skill test results are going down for underprivileged kids—another example of the widening gap between have and have-not children and teenagers, particularly in the United States. Competition for spots at the top universities and graduate and professional programs in Canada and the United States has never been stiffer.

The generation born since the late 1970s has a closer affinity with their parents than their boomer parents had with their own. Most have been raised by dual-career moms and dads. Until the most recent war in Iraq, there had been no anti-war movement to crystallize the rebellion of boomers' kids from their parents, and the anti-war, anti-Bush protesters of recent years have just as likely been middle-aged liberals as pro-peace teens. Boomer kids do not espouse free love, and they are just as likely as their parents are to debate abortion rights or same-sex marriage. Though unfazed today by the pill, a novelty for the boomer, they are relatively cautious and concerned about sexually transmitted diseases.

Today's teens and 20-somethings have tremendous economic clout, especially in the United States. Like their parents, they represent a demographic tidal wave in the United States that will help shape trends, attitudes, and commerce for much of the first half of the 21st century.

KEY POINTS

- While economic developments cause significant demographic changes, demographic shifts also have significant economic consequences.

- Boomer parents (born 1901 to 1945) have strong and vocal lobbying power.

- As children of the Depression and wartime, they are more frugal than their children.

- Boomers (born 1946 to the mid-1960s) grew up in times of economic bounty and represent huge buying power. They created the housing boom and brought home ownership to record levels.

- Early boomers were the first in their generation to enter schools, the job market, and the housing market. They benefited from being the first in.

- Late boomers had very different life experiences and have found it tougher to amass wealth.

- Generation X (born 1966 to 1976) is a relatively small generation and must wait for the boomers' jobs to become available to climb the corporate ladder.

- Generation Y (born after 1976) are the children of the boomers and Gen Xers. Gen Y is roughly equivalent in size to the boomer generation in Canada, as fertility rates fell to an average of just 1.5 children per woman.

- In the United States, where fertility rates are at a 30-year high of 2.1, the number of people under the age of 30 is far greater than the number of boomers. They are the next big American population cohort and have enormous economic clout.

Chapter 3

Health and Achievement: The Keys for Successful Retirement

Today's boomers are the first generation to grow up with childhood vaccines, antibiotics, and, for the most part, much better nutrition than in the past. Childhood was easier for the boomers than it was for their parents. In addition, they have suffered far less exposure to health risks at work. This bodes very well for healthy middle and old age, with fewer infirmities and less pain and misery. Most boomers stand a good chance of living longer, healthier lives than did previous generations. It is common for boomers in late middle age to have no chronic health problems, and many expect to live as long as 30 years in retirement.

Before our parents' generation, people worked until they died or until they were so disabled they couldn't carry on. In 1890, nearly everyone died while still working, and if they were healthy enough not to expire on the job, they retired at about age 85.[1]

Now, the average age of retirement is 61 in Canada and 62 in the United States. This certainly raises a question about why we retire so young, and suggests that retirement ages could well rise considerably in coming decades.

While the median age of retirement in Canada is 61, a 2002 survey found that almost 20 percent of working people don't plan to retire at all.[2] Statistics Canada reports that it sees so many people *transitioning* into retirement today that it is becoming difficult to define what retirement really is. There may no longer be a typical retirement age. Similarly, in the United States, surveys suggest that most working adults hope to work in retirement, with many looking for part-time jobs or for opportunities to move in and out of the workforce. Bob Willis, a professor of economics at the University of Michigan, found that the percentage of men and women in their early 50s who expected to work past 65 increased between 1992 and 2004 (the last year for which the data are available), and anecdotal data suggest the trend has continued in both the United States and Canada.[3]

Life expectancy continues to rise, and—given coming developments in biotechnology—boomer kids will more commonly live to be 100. A retirement age of 65 was first set in 1916 by German chancellor Otto von Bismarck (he had earlier set it at 70, in 1889); and when age 65 was adopted by President Roosevelt in 1935 for the United States' Social Security system, average life expectancy was no more than 62, and for men it was 57.[4] Very few people actually retired.

A recent U.S. study of the body dimensions and health of individual Union soldiers in the American Civil War and their direct descendants found that people today are taller, heavier, and healthier than they were in the 1860s. They do not suffer early in life from the chronic conditions that used to be so prevalent among the young.[5] There is less disability among older people today as well. Even the human mind has improved, as IQ levels have been rising for decades, and the chance of having dementia in old age appears to have fallen in recent years.

While we have often attributed this to better medical care and advanced techniques such as cataract surgery, joint replacements, and medications to reduce blood pressure or cholesterol levels, recent research suggests that it is the improvements in pre- and post-natal nutrition up to the age of two, as well as vaccinations that prevent some key childhood diseases, that have yielded these health dividends later in life.

Studies in Sweden, Finland, France, Britain, and the Netherlands also indicate the importance of pre- and post-natal care, and there is evidence that improving this care in the developing world is leading to healthier adults and rising life expectancy there as well. In 1900, 13 percent of the people who made it to 65 could expect to live to 85. Today, nearly *half* could expect to celebrate their 85th birthday. In 1900, people age 50 with reasonably good health could expect to live 21 more years. In 2003, they could expect to live 31 more years. Indeed—another surprising statistic—*there are more people alive today over the age of 85 than have ever lived to that age in the history of humankind.*

Health Care and the Aging Boomer

The one thing most boomers seem to have in common is an aversion to growing old, which in part helps explain their reluctance to plan for their elderly future. Surveys suggest that boomers feel much younger than they are.[6] They don't consider themselves "middle aged" until around 50 to 55 and would not want to be described as "senior" until age 70 or beyond. It's often said that

"50 is the new 40, and 60 is the new 50," and so on up the line. With the rise in life expectancy, this may well be valid.

But one trend causing concern is the surge in obesity. Healthy aging is at risk for some boomers, as the links between obesity, increased incidence of disease, and lower life expectancy are well established.[7] According to recent data, 23 percent of Canadian and 30 percent of American adults are obese.[8]

Obesity is not only a boomer problem. It is starting earlier in life, and a very troubling 8 percent of Canadian children and 15 percent of U.S. children are now obese. This raises the incidence of diabetes and coronary disease, as well as breast and colon cancer and even dementia, which is a huge burden on the already overtaxed health-care system (Table 1).[9]

The World Health Organization estimates that premature deaths associated with diabetes, coronary heart disease, and

Table 1

Medical Complications of Obesity

Coronary Heart Disease	
Cancer	breast, uterus, cervix, colon, esophagus, pancreas, kidney, prostrate
Stroke	
Pulmonary Disease	abnormal function, obstructive sleep apnea, hypoventilation syndrome
Nonalcoholic Fatty Liver Disease	steatosis, steatohepatitis, cirrhosis
Gynecologic Abnormalities	abnormal menses, infertility, polycycstic ovarian syndrome
Phlebitis	venous stasis
Gall Bladder Disease	
Severe Pancreatitis	
Osteoarthritis	
Skin Disease	
Cataracts	
Gout	
Headaches	

Reprinted with permission of NAASO, the Obesity Society.

cancer will cause $9 billion of lost income in Canada in 2015.[10] Health care is among the fastest-growing sectors in Canada and the United States. The aging population alone will increase the proportion of relative health-care expenditures in developed economies, while the rise will be exacerbated by the increasing tendency toward obesity in boomers and their kids in virtually every G8 country.

It is not only older women with osteoporosis who become too frail to live unassisted, but also the growing number of obese seniors. Dr. Samuel Klein, a professor of nutrition and medicine at the Washington University School of Medicine, has reported that since 1990 the incidence of obesity in older adults has grown to a monstrous 50 percent.[11] Their much-reduced muscle mass leads to frailty and the need for premature long-term care. Even moderate weight loss and increased activity makes a big difference.

Obesity is negatively correlated with education and financial well-being.[12] The better educated and the wealthier the individual, the less likely it is that he or she will be obese. Mississippi, for example, continued to lead the way: An estimated 29.5 percent of adults there are considered obese. The five states with the highest obesity rates—Mississippi, Alabama, West Virginia, Louisiana, and Kentucky—also exhibit much higher rates of poverty than the national norm. In Canada, a similar relationship exists, with the East Coast generally posting the highest rates of obesity and the highest poverty rates in the country.

The wealthier regions of Canada boast the highest number of fitness clubs, organic and health food stores, and the largest proportion of middle-aged "fitness freaks." In the United States, the five states with the lowest obesity—Colorado, Hawaii, Massachusetts, Rhode Island, and Vermont—are relatively well off, and I've heard it said that the thinnest region of the United States is the Upper East Side of New York City, where wealthy matrons pop diet pills prescribed by their Park Avenue doctors. Thin is chic among the rich. Even too thin is chic in some circles, as evidenced by the anorexic models of the fashion runways.

Extremes in body weight are prevalent among all age groups. Ironically, while obesity is rampant, the incidence of anorexia and bulimia is also rising, among young women (and even young men), the middle-aged, and the elderly. People are more diet-conscious than ever, but even so, Americans and Canadians are also, on average, more overweight than ever.

Before the turn of the 20th century, death was often due to illnesses resulting from grossly poor nutrition and to bacterial infections. We overcame significant illnesses when it was recognized that severe nutrient deficiencies could cause them; for example, scurvy (caused by a vitamin C deficiency) and rickets (a vitamin D deficiency). Then, around the Second World War, we discovered a way to fight infection, another major killer, through penicillin and other antibiotics. Now we find ourselves with illness and disease again related to poor nutrition—generally poor eating—which is "malnutrition" of a different sort: too many fats; too many or too few calories; empty calories; too many toxins; and too much processed food with additives such as processed sugars, chemicals, antibiotics, and hormones. In the end, it is malnutrition that is the common thread between being too fat and too thin. Hence we are seeing widespread cardiovascular disease, cancer, diabetes, osteoporosis, and allergies. Today's stressful, always-rushing lifestyle also contributes to these infirmities. People often graze or snack rather than eat well-balanced meals. Convenience becomes more important than nutrition.

Eating well and exercising appropriately is relatively expensive, and it requires an awareness and appreciation of nutrition and fitness. Fast food, pop, and candy—all "empty-calorie" foods as a general group, with little in the way of nutrition—are a lot cheaper than grilled fish, cruciferous vegetables, and fresh fruit, but they pack a hefty wallop in the calorie department. Sadly, only 15.6 percent of the U.S population has health insurance (59.8 percent of which is employment-based coverage and 27.3 percent is government-program insurance).[13] Those who are least likely to have health insurance in the United States, or access to a family doctor in Canada, are the most likely to need it, and need it now. Instead, their health care is generally symptoms-based; in other words, received only after problems have begun to manifest themselves. Their most common route through the medical system is the emergency room and other ad hoc facilities. By this time, disease is often too advanced to cure, and certainly far more expensive to treat. Exposure to preventive medicine is rare among the lower-income strata of Canada and the United States.

The Weaker Sex?

Life expectancy for women is still several years longer than it is for men. In Canada, the average life expectancy for men is 77 years and for women 82 years. American men have an average life expectancy at birth of 75.2 years (only 69.8 years for African-American men), compared with 80.4 years for women overall. For just about every one of the leading causes of death—from cancer to influenza and pneumonia, chronic liver disease, diabetes, and AIDS—men die younger than women. Cancer strikes one in two men, compared to one in three women. In part, this is because more men than women smoke, and possibly also because of occupational exposures. One notable exception is Alzheimer's disease: more women than men die of it. More women die of breast cancer than do men of prostate cancer: 5,300 Canadian women died of breast cancer in 2006, compared with 4,200 deaths of men from prostate cancer. The ratio is similar in the United States, as almost 41,000 American women died of breast cancer versus 27,350 deaths from prostate cancer.

Many expected the gender-longevity gap to change with the entry of women into the workforce. As women were confronted with the same career stresses faced by men, the theory went, women would be just as prone to the illnesses of premature aging—heart disease, stroke, and cancer. But this has not happened. The real inequality of the sexes is illustrated in Chart 9: The number of males in the U.S. population exceeds the number of females until the mid-30s age group, and then, as life progresses, the number of males falls sharply, and turns parabolically downward as men approach 70.[14] The Canadian male-to-female ratio follows a similar pattern. According to the latest census in the United States (in 2005), nearly 44 percent of women age 65 and older are widowed. For men in the same age range, the proportion is only 13 percent; similar percentages are evident in Canada as well.

Men's greater vulnerability appears to start quite early. More male foetuses are conceived, but they are at greater risk of miscarriage and stillbirth. As infants, newborn boys have a higher rate of mortality. As children, boys are at higher risk for developmental disabilities and autism. Boys and men are more likely to be colour-blind and suffer higher rates of hearing loss. They are believed to have weaker immune systems and may also recover more slowly from illnesses.[15]

As I mentioned earlier, the most recent data available (for 2003/04) show that the incidence of heart disease, diabetes, and

Chart 9

Men at Greater Risk from Aging
Males per 100 Females—2005

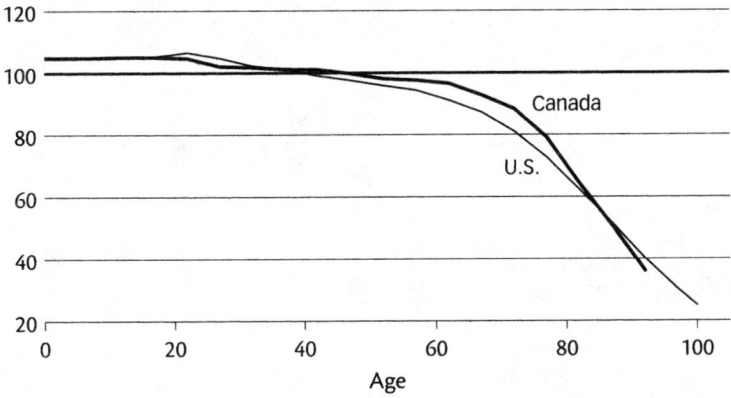

Sources: Statistics Canada, U.S. Census Bureau, National Center for Health Statistics.

cancer in people age 50 and over is significantly higher for men than it is for women. One explanation is that women take better care of themselves (Chart 10). Women are more likely to see a doctor for an annual checkup or when they suffer unexplained symptoms. They are also more likely to follow their doctors' orders, take the drugs their physicians prescribe, and are even more likely than men, by a small margin, to have a flu shot.

Women read more about fitness and nutrition. They are generally in control of the grocery shopping, and hence more likely to buy foods they like that are good for them. They are more apt to take supplements, exercise, and eat right. Women are more inclined than men to join a health club and use that membership. Many clubs are now geared specifically to women, and not just 20-somethings in skimpy workout clothes, but 50- or 60-something women endowed with a wider girth and

Chart 10

Women More Attentive to Health Care
United States (percent)

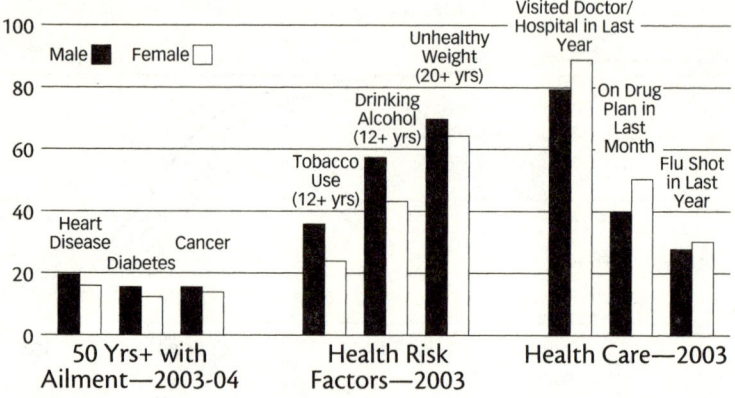

Sources: United States Census Bureau, National Center for Health Statistics.

thicker middle who look nothing like the stick-thin models in the magazines. The for-females-only Curves chain caters to such women, with fewer mirrors and simple 30-minute exercise routines. The growing number of health sections in newspapers, health shows, and segments on TV, and the countless websites on health-related issues, enjoy predominantly female audiences.

Women are also less dare-devilish than men. They are more likely to wear their seatbelts and to stick to the speed limit. They are less apt to experiment with drugs or to drink excessively. Women are also more likely to use sunblock, more so even than men diagnosed with skin cancer or melanoma. It is estimated that as of 2003, nearly 36 percent of men over age 12 still smoke, while only 24 percent of women do so. When it comes to weight, the differences are smaller but still significant: just under 70 percent of men age 20 and older are at an unhealthy weight, compared to 64 percent of women, stunningly high numbers in both cases.

Men also suffer more accidental deaths and serious injuries and are more likely to die of their injuries. They are 3 times as likely to be victims of a homicide, 4 times as likely to commit suicide, and, as teenagers, 11 times as likely to drown. Some experts suggest that some of this reckless behaviour might stem from the increased incidence of undiagnosed depression in men. Women and girls are much more likely to seek psychiatric help and take antidepressants. Women show more emotion, and so may be more aware of what they are feeling. Men are socialized to believe they are bullet-proof, and vulnerability is seen as a sign of weakness.

As a result, even though more baby boys are born, women outnumber men among people in their mid-30s. Among people age 100, women outnumber men by eight to one.[16]

What these statistics suggest is that most women will outlive their male partners—which is all the more reason why women should understand their household finances and have a large-enough nest egg and long-term insurance to assure comfort and security in later years. Most women will spend a significant number of years living alone, with other women, or with younger family members. Indeed, according to the 2005 U.S. census, 47 percent of women age 20 and over report they are living without a spouse, up from 34 percent in 1950.[17] Too many are still phobic about finances; that needs to change or they will be prey to unscrupulous advisers or greedy heirs. Women have good reason to take care of themselves well before their elder years to assure an active, *independent*, and healthful old age.

The Crucial Shift from Late-Disease Care to Health Preservation[18]

An estimated 70 percent of the health-care dollar is spent on finding and dealing with late disease—yet it is far less expensive and far easier to cure early-stage disease. Much more emphasis, including research and development, should be focused on prevention, prediction, and education so individuals can be better informed about their particular health risks early enough in life to do something about them. The health-care system must shift from chronic care to early detection and prevention.[19] We can now determine our predisposition to virtually all of the major causes of premature death and chronic disabilities—including diabetes, heart disease, stroke, osteoporosis, cancer, dementia, and some autoimmune conditions—through newly developing diagnostic and genetic testing—including blood, hair, saliva, and waste-matter analysis, scans, which are increasingly precise, investigation of family and individual health history, knowledge of current habits, diet, and lifestyle occupational conditions such as stress, job anxiety, 24/7 work, and insufficient true-vacation time.

With this knowledge, nutritional, physical, lifestyle, and medical interventions can be taken to at least mitigate these risks and assure that your life is not unnecessarily shortened or burdened with infirmity. This is a new and different kind of health care, where individuals are proactive and responsible for helping to determine their own well-being.

Dr. Lewis Kuller, professor and past chair of the department of epidemiology at the University of Pittsburgh's School of Public Health, believes fully in the power of prevention to markedly reduce chronic disease. Even if we were to apply what we already know about the causes of disease, it would significantly reduce morbidity and disability. But we are ineffective in the application of this knowledge—prevention policy is poor. According to Dr. Kuller, "We know that a 50-year-old man or woman who is a non-smoker and has LDL [the so-called "bad cholesterol"] below 100 and blood pressure of 120 or lower has a very high chance of a healthy life and living to age 85."[20]

Education in primary prevention is vital. Sorely lacking is public policy to teach and apply what we need to know about healthy eating, nutritional supplements, fitness, environmental toxins, stress, and other psychological factors that can be toxic. We know the general public is very interested in these issues based upon the amount of attention they receive in the popular media. But without concerted effort and access to information, much of what we hear is anecdotal and often incomplete and misleading.

Virtually all health-care systems are missing the expert who can assess the complete health scorecard for each individual—nutritional status, fitness, genetic risks, physical and mental health, social and environmental factors, and work and family issues. And no health insurance, be it public or private, would cover all the tests required to do a thorough job using state-of-the-art techniques. Yet in the long run it would greatly reduce the cost of health care.

For example, studies show that the incidence of breast cancer is lower in women who in adolescence engaged in sports, dance, gymnastics, or athletic activities. Knowing that at middle age doesn't do us much good, but teaching it to our daughters and granddaughters does. Risks are also reduced with pregnancy before the age of 35, breast feeding, maintaining appropriate body weight, as well as adult fitness activity. Even for those women who have a genetic predisposition to breast or ovarian cancer, similar recommendations are valid and, in addition, earlier and more frequent self- and medical examination are warranted—including mammograms, bone density CT scans, capsule endoscopy, magnetic resonance imaging (MRI), and ultrasound—to provide the best chance that disease is caught in its earliest stages.

There are now blood tests that help to signal the possible onset of prostate or ovarian cancer. The use of preventive and diagnostic genetics can not only give early warning but also determine the appropriate protocols for prevention and treatment. Research suggests that cancer risk can be reduced by appropriate diet and nutritional supplementation. It has been known for some time that diet and stress have a meaningful effect on coronary risk and stroke. Appropriate diet and physical activity can mitigate the need for insulin injections in some Type II diabetics and smartly reduce the devastating side effects of diabetes on all of the body's systems. Mental activity can reduce the risk or delay the onset of Alzheimer's, as can B vitamins, vitamin E, and anti-inflammatory drugs; this disease has also been linked to the ingestion of certain metals and to obesity. Excessive levels of toxins in the blood can now be detected by a blood test that also measures the level of certain nutrients and amino acids.

Research suggests that increasing one's intake of vitamin D through moderate exposure to sunlight and eating certain foods can help prevent osteoporosis, and according to the latest studies vitamin D is also believed to reduce the incidence of prostate, colon, and breast cancer by as much as 60 percent. With the publication of virtually every new medical journal, more information becomes available about the possible association between specific diseases and everyday behaviours or environmental toxins.

Ideally, preventive health care would be practised by all. Technological developments are making this easier. With the ability now to assess an individual's risk factors, actions can be taken that will dramatically extend and improve quality of life. The application of digital technology has also improved detection and diagnosis methods, which help to catch disease in its earliest stages, when treatment options are much better, less invasive, and less costly, and mortality rates are lower. Positron emission tomography (PET) and computerized tomography (CT), along with MRI scans, can painlessly see the spread of cancer in the body to determine the appropriate treatment. These scans can gauge the effectiveness of the treatment within four days, greatly improving the prospects of successful care. Joe Hogan, president of GE Healthcare, estimates that early-stage breast cancer costs the U.S. health-care system roughly US$10,000 to US$15,000 for treatment. If it is found in its late stage, however, when it has already metastasized, it costs roughly US$60,000 to US$145,000, and, of course, treatment is less effective.[21]

When it comes to cardiovascular disease—which is the biggest killer here and in most of the developed world—treatment of early-stage high cholesterol or hypertension costs the medical system roughly US$1,000 to US$1,500 per patient, whereas late-stage treatment might start at about US$30,000 and rise to more than US$50,000 for coronary bypass surgery.

As Joe Hogan says, the goal is to "treat as early as you can and as minimally invasively as possible"; non-invasive surgery is now available for fibroids, gall bladder problems, liver disease, and some prostate conditions. *You should make the effort to find disease early and deal with it; focus on keeping yourself healthy and productive.* But you have to be proactive and take responsibility for your own preventive health plan. Some of this might be costly, as many tests are not covered by government health insurance or even available yet in Canada. This presents another reason why we must be financially prepared for the later decades of our lives; appropriate medical and lifestyle interventions can help secure a healthy, happy old age.

We know that chronic diseases associated with aging will soon dominate the health-care system. By far the most money spent on health care is in the last two years of life, when prevention is no longer possible and much of the care is palliative (Chart 11). Even now, chronic diseases affect about one-half of the population. But it doesn't have to be this way.

What I am describing is more than an add-on to today's medical care. It is a truly new system with far different emphases and responsibilities, and far-reaching benefits. But there are major impediments to the move toward prevention, health preservation, and early detection. And the greatest of these are within the health-care system itself.

Chart 11

Annual Health-Care Spending by Age
(US$000s per capita)

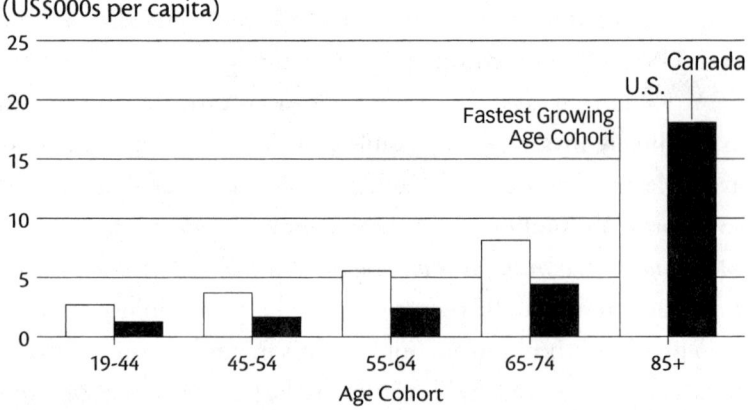

Sources: Milken Institute, 1999 (U.S.), Health Canada, 2000–01 (1.5 C$/US$).

There is no incentive in any system in favour of preventive behaviour. In public-health systems, hospitals have little incentive to maximize the efficacy of treatment at minimum costs. Hospitals cannot create profits for investment in capital equipment and trained personnel, and doctors are paid by the visit. The more patients doctors see, the more money they make (although in Canada, some physicians have been subject to a clawback of income over a specified level, which of course reduces the supply of medical services). This encourages doctors to see as many patients as possible in a day, which only shortens each visit and encourages symptom-based rather than prevention-based treatment and advice. Doctors have little time to educate their patients about preventive measures, and many of them do not keep up with the rapid developments in preventive care and diagnostics. As well, doctors are far too likely to prescribe drugs than work with patients to make lifestyle and nutrition changes; and many physicians prescribe surgical or other interventions before less invasive and more natural protocols are given a chance to be effective.

Patients, as well, should be "paid" to be healthy, with reduced prices for health-care insurance and life insurance, some of which is happening already. Smokers pay more for life insurance, but the same could apply for such characteristics as obesity, inactivity, or other controllable unhealthy behaviour. Better still, pay people for losing weight, eating right, and exercising through government incentive programs. Some businesses in the United States are already doing this by encouraging workers to meet health goals with monetary remuneration. Private and public partnerships could provide the flexibility needed for people to take care of themselves at reasonable cost, even during the working day. There is nothing like a noon workout to boost energy levels and reduce stress.

The food industry contributes to unhealthy eating with additives and high fat, salt, and sugar content in its products; they make them taste better, so people buy more. And even though sugar-free, carb-free, and fat-free products are everywhere, there is still a growing obesity problem. Just because a certain cake might be fat free, it doesn't mean it is calorie free—and often the fat-free label is a licence for people to eat more. The full disclosure you now find on food packaging declaring calorie, fat, protein, vitamin, and fibre content is an important step in the right direction. Take the time to read the labels and understand what the nutritional contents mean. Demand healthier, good-tasting, appealing food.

The Wellness Boom

There is a rapidly growing sector that can loosely be identified as "wellness lifestyle," which includes spas, traditional and alternative medicine, behavioural therapy, spirituality, fitness, nutrition, and beauty. As more people demand a holistic approach to feeling well and operating at peak performance into their 80s or 90s, this sector will only expand. Whole residential areas are now developing around the concept of wellness and boast spas, fitness centres, and medical facilities. And the medical clinics themselves will no longer simply treat disease, but assess, detect, and mitigate health risks and coach people along the way to maximum wellness.[22]

More and more boomers are searching for peace of mind, enduring happiness, and a sense of connectedness to other people; this search has no doubt been made more urgent, at least in part, by the frightening state of the world, from terrorism to environmental degradation. Meditation, yoga, tai chi, and spirituality—be it through organized religion, the belief in a higher spirit or nuturing of the soul, or a connection with nature—are already a growing part of what it takes to manage stress, solve problems, and enhance wellness. The mind-body connection is now well established in traditional medical circles, and boomers recognize that stress can kill. Lingering anger, resentment, and jealousy are corrosive to the human body. Depression is a contributing factor of dementia. The compulsive and unbounded need to compete and win, rather than collaborate and help others, eventually leads to mental and physical burnout.

There is bountiful evidence that focusing holistically on wellness can reduce health-care costs by emphasizing prevention over treatment, and a growing number of employers now promote wellness at work, both to cut costs and to reduce stress and health-related absenteeism. But one of the roots of today's health-care crisis is that prevention and care are not suitably integrated.

The desire to reduce health-care costs is one force behind the rise of the wellness industry; the other is the growing demand from consumers for things that make them feel better. Increasingly, older boomers want to feel more "balanced." This is a big change in boomer psychology. At 35, we were the hard-driving crowd that postponed just about everything to achieve career success. Market research suggests that today's 35-year-olds have a much stronger desire to lead healthy, balanced lifestyles. They've learned from seeing the burnout and premature ailments of boomers, not to mention the cost to family and society.

But even the most driven boomers are now seeing the value in taking time to improve their health and create a sense of contentment. As older boomers return for their 40-year university reunions, they are a much less competitive and self-centred bunch than they were in their early careers. We are becoming wise enough to know that money or status does not define enduring success.

Success in work is not equivalent to success in life—something that boomer kids might appreciate more than their parents.

Success in life is multidimensional. Partly, it results from accomplishment and mastery, but forces beyond our control also come into play. Success is never a straight upward trajectory; often it is determined by our ability to bounce back from failure and adversity. Success can mean significant material reward, but it can also represent moral achievements. Success is admired by society, providing a sense of belonging—but the admiration might come late or even posthumously; to the extent success brings pleasure, it can cause happiness.[23] Professors Laura Nash and Howard Stevenson at the Harvard Business School succinctly define success as a personal and enduring concept: *"Enduring success is the collection of activities that will be viewed affirmatively by you and those you care about—now, throughout your life, and beyond."*[24]

This suggests that each of us must define success for ourselves; this is a process involving many aspects of our lives, not a single, one-time definition. For goal achievement to be truly satisfying it must involve growth and expanded capacity—causing you to stretch your capabilities and horizons. Goals must be meaningful and important to you. Some goals should be of social significance, having a sustained impact on others you care about.

Boomers in their retirement years will add to their collection of personal successes, doing things that a full-time career and family demands might not have allowed. But even during your working years, reaching the top in business or a profession is rarely the measure of lasting success. Other activities are also important, such as creating a happy and functional household, raising self-confident and independent children with a high sense of moral values, giving and receiving from friends, helping others, mentoring, doing community service, and leaving a legacy. This requires trade-offs. Being the best at one activity but a failure at others that are also important to you will not likely lead to sustained happiness.

There is always someone or something around the corner that will knock you out of the top spot. Imagine if Olympic gold medalists felt a sense of failure or anger when younger athletes beat their records. It is impossible for an individual to remain on top, and the need to do so will only lead to fear and envy. There will always be someone richer, faster, or more innovative coming down the pike; and it is healthy for different goals to grow in importance at different stages of life. Great athletes retire younger than most of us, and many find it difficult. Those who adapt best have other goals to add to their success in life. They are not "over the hill"; they are at a new plateau that allows them to broaden their outlook and to help others.

Boomers who are successful in life feel a sense of making a difference, of lasting achievement, and of helping others. This requires contributions beyond the workplace, and as boomers age they have the opportunity to make these contributions. Many boomers are realizing that there comes a time when they have enough in the way of material success. Something deeper and more spiritual is beginning to motivate a growing number of boomers, and with our longer lifespan we have the opportunity to achieve so much more than earlier generations did. It is the combination of these dimensions that will create a successful retirement.

KEY POINTS

- Boomers will *transition* into retirement, taking on new challenges.

- The increase in longevity provides the opportunity for boomers to do so much more than earlier generations did.

- Obesity threatens the longevity of many.

- Women should be prepared to live without a partner for a significant number of years, given the gender-longevity gap.

- Disease prevention is key to a successful retirement. More is available today than ever before to determine and mitigate your health risks.

- There is no reason to resolve yourself to chronic disease conditions. Late-life can be active and pain-free. You can be accepting of natural physical and mental weakening, while enjoying the enhanced wisdom, selflessness, and peacefulness that aging can bring.

- Many causes of premature death can now be avoided, but it requires you to be well informed and proactive in your health preservation.

- Elder boomers are in a period in their lives when they want to give back to the community and create a lasting legacy.

- Success in life varies from person to person, but it is much broader than simply success in work.

- Boomers will use their retirement years to enhance their success in life.

- Successful retirement encompasses activities that achieve something of value to you, give you pleasure, connect with other people of all ages, and is of lasting value. It also requires an acceptance of change, some of which will be painful.

Chapter 4

Canadian Boomers in a Global Context

Canada is too dependent on the strength of economic activity and financial flows in the rest of the world—not just in the United States, but increasingly Asia as well—for the future of Canadian boomers to be discussed in geographical isolation. The surge in oil and metals prices that triggered the dramatic rise in the Canadian dollar, the booming housing market, and the plunge in unemployment was largely caused by the double-digit growth in China. While the United States remains our number-one trading partner, the rapidly growing middle class in the developing world is providing enormous benefit and opportunity to Canadians.

Imports from China have helped increase the purchasing power of Canadian households and businesses, and Chinese demand for our products increases the value of the Canadian dollar, our corporate profits, stock prices on the Toronto Stock Exchange (TSX), and the real value of Canadian incomes. To be sure, there are losers in this process; many Canadian manufacturers could not compete with low-wage producers, especially as the loonie strengthened. But adjustment has always been part of economic development, and judging from the strength of our economy and the more than 16 years of uninterrupted economic expansion, Canada is certainly up to the challenge.

Boomers will benefit in their financial and lifestyle planning from a broad understanding of the general trends in the global economy and how they influence Canada. We begin by taking a brief look at the demographics of the rest of the world.

Younger Than the Rest of the G8

Canada has proportionately the second largest youth market in the G8, and the population of both Canada and the United States will be augmented by increasing immigration. There is a larger pool of young workers available to replace retirees in the United States than there is in Canada, Japan, Germany, France, Italy, and the countries of the former Soviet Union. The U.S. fertility rate, at 2.1 children per woman, is consistent with a relatively stable population level. The American populace, however, will continue to age as life expectancy rises; the number of people over the age of 85 is growing much more rapidly than other age cohorts in all of the developed countries.

While the U.S. and Canadian populations are aging, populations in other areas of the world are aging even faster and will be facing some of the more harsh implications of a maturing society sooner. Fertility rates in most industrialized nations have trended downward for decades, and this is now becoming a serious economic problem. The fertility rate in the European Union (EU) is even lower than in Canada. According to the Population Reference Bureau, a non-profit foundation that collects global demographic data, Uganda's population is likely to more than quadruple to 130 million by 2050, while Germany's numbers are projected to decline by 9 percent, from 82 million to 75 million, over the same period.[1]

While 20 percent of the Japanese population is aged 65 and older, and about 16 percent of Europeans are elderly, only 12.3 percent of the U.S. population is 65 and older, and in Canada the share is 13 percent (Chart 12).[2] The average age of Europeans and Japanese is higher, and it is rising faster. Japan's population is *aged* and *aging*. Indeed, Japanese men and women, on average, have the highest life expectancy in the world at age 86 for women and 79 for men, and their average fertility rate is

Chart 12

U.S. a Spring Chicken Compared to Most
Population Aged 65 or Older – 2005 (% of total population)

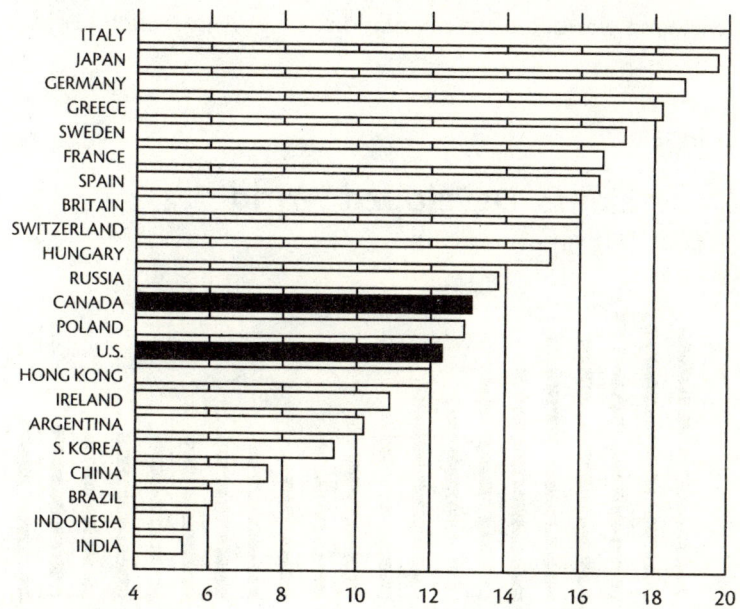

Source: World Bank.

only 1.29. The countries of the former Soviet Union are also aged and aging relative to Canada and the United States.

Looking at the dependency ratio—defined as young and old as a percentage of the working-age population—the elderly will far outnumber youth in the developed world in the next decade (Chart 13). Indeed, in the history of the world, *50 percent of all the people that have been alive at age 65 and older are alive today.* Many of these older people are living in a state of diminished health, which puts a huge burden on the health-care system that will only increase in the future.

Much Older Than Most Developing Countries

Most of the developing world, however, is far younger than the developed world, and its populations are growing much faster. In

Chart 13

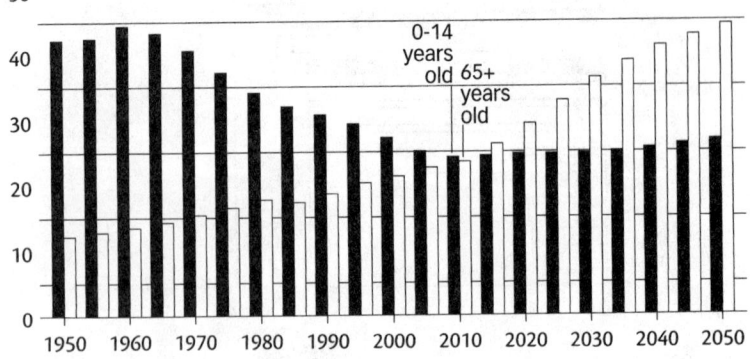

Dependents: Developed World
(% of working age population)

Source: United Nations Population Division.

the developing world, the key dependents are children, as there are far more people under the age of 14 than over the age of 65 (Chart 14). India is a great example. China, on the other hand, is an exception; owing to the introduction of the one-child policy in the 1970s, the population in China is older and slower-growing than it is in other developing countries. About 8 percent of the 1.3 billion people in China are aged 65 and over—high by developing-world standards. The International Labour Organization predicts that by 2013, India will have more young workers aged 20 to 24 than will China, and will surpass China in total population by 2030.[3] This means that, in time, India's economy will grow more rapidly than China's, boosting the relative prospects of business development in India and other relatively young developing economies.

China is increasingly aware of the unintended consequences of their efforts at population-control. Because Chinese parents

Chart 14

Dependents: Developing World
(% of working age population)

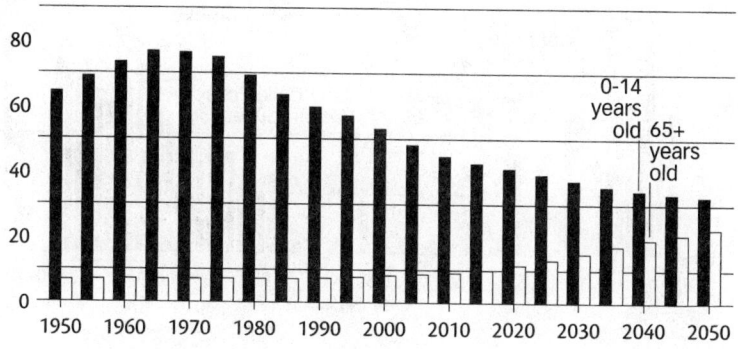

Source: United Nations Population Division.

traditionally prefer to have a boy if they can have only one child, the number of young girls relative to boys has fallen sharply (Chart 15). In a significant number of cases, babies have been given up for international adoption. However, the supply of girls for adoption is diminishing, apparently because ultrasound has allowed pregnant women to detect the sex of their foetus early enough to abort.

China has vowed to control the gender imbalance by cracking down on the epidemic of abortions of female foetuses, and in May 2006 the director of China's National Population and Family Planning Commission called for the criminalization of sex identification by ultrasound.[4] But social problems have already developed because of the gender imbalance. Many young men cannot find a wife; there are simply too few to go around. Over the next two decades, as many as 40 million young Chinese men will not find a mate and will therefore not settle down and have

Chart 15

It's a Man's World in China
(number of males born for every 100 females)

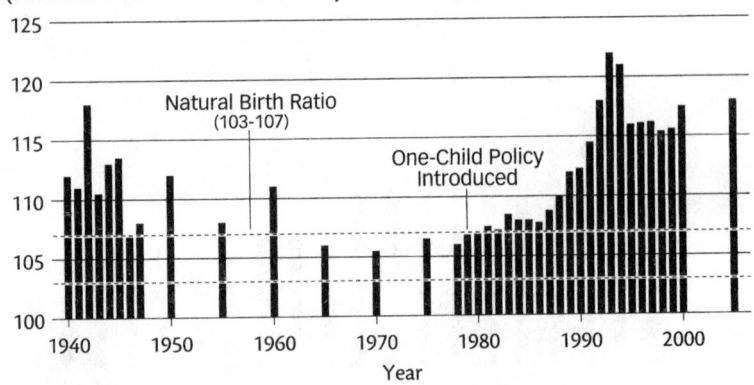

Source: Report of National Fertility and Family Planning Survey.

children. The Chinese see this as a threat to social order. Most violent crimes are committed by young unmarried males who lack stable social bonds, and high male-to-female ratios historically trigger violence, both domestic and international.

Developing Economy Growth Is a Blessing for Canada

In the past 30 years, billions of people have become a part of the global "free-trade" economy, increasing sharply the demand for the products and services that Canada produces, which in turn has boosted the value of Canadian financial assets. For boomers planning for retirement, this is great news. The rise in the loonie has increased the value of the money we earn and the money we invest; the real purchasing power of Canadians has risen. We are richer today relative to other countries than we have been in decades, and our continued competitive advantage in high-skilled manufacturing, mining, and technical services bodes well for our future financial security.

Beginning in 1978, China has gradually shifted from a government-controlled to a market-driven economy, bringing 1.3 billion people into global labour force and consumer markets. With the dismantling of the Berlin Wall in 1989 and breakup of the Soviet Union in 1991, millions more joined them. The supply of labour and the demand for goods and services have, therefore, grown dramatically. Never before has so much of the world's population been under the capitalist system with the relatively free trade of goods and services on a global basis. This, in combination with the evolution of digital technology, the mass availability of personal computers and the internet, and improvements in transportation, has triggered globalization.

These changes have dramatically increased competition world-wide. Workers in the formerly Communist economies are paid far lower wages than their counterparts are in the industrial world, giving manufacturers a strong competitive advantage in the production of labour-intensive, low-skill products. Demand for these inexpensive imports has surged, reducing the pricing power of their Western competitors and contributing to a substantial decline in inflation and, therefore, interest rates. Stepped-up competition led many corporations to move production to these low-cost regions, especially China. Manufacturing surged, and the Chinese economy boomed. The goods that China supplies have fallen in price as the prices of the goods China demands have risen. On balance, this has had a disinflationary influence on the global economy.

Commodities are among the goods that China demands, and most commodity prices have surged. Emerging economies are about twice as commodity-intensive as advanced, knowledge-intensive economies are; they use roughly twice the volume of energy and industrial materials for every additional dollar of gross domestic product (GDP) than in developed countries. This has created significant excess demand for many materials and indus-trial resources—most notably oil and base metals. The oil and mining industries did little exploration and development in the past few decades to increase supply, and it is only since the prices of these products have risen sharply that development has become economically viable. It will take years for supply to catch up with demand.

For many industrial materials, China is the number-one or -two consumer and importer in the world. No wonder the price of oil, copper, zinc, uranium, gold, and other commodities has jumped for most of this decade. This has been reflected in a relative surge in the commodity-heavy stock markets and currencies, Canada's among them.

Emerging economies are growing far more rapidly than are large industrial economies, as farm workers move into the cities, labour-force growth surges in the factory sector, and income per capita rises, resulting in a rapidly growing middle class. As much as 60 percent of global growth could come from developing countries in the next decade, compared to only about 20 percent in the past decade. The developed economies will rely increasingly on these growth centres for their expanding consumer and business markets, and for their young and relatively inexpensive labour.

China and other countries with large trade surpluses with the United States have funnelled their U.S. dollar profits and foreign exchange reserves into the U.S. Treasury bond and bill markets, helping to keep interest rates low. Rates are even lower still in Canada, owing to our better trade and government balances (both in surplus), lower inflation, and stronger currency. As boomers and boomer parents in Canada and the United States are confronted with historically low yields on government bonds, they are willingly taking more risk in their investment portfolios to pick up higher returns, moving into corporate bonds, junk bonds, and even emerging-market debt. Dividend-paying stocks and other income-producing equity investments, as well as growth stocks and commodity stocks, are also popular investments for boomers, providing higher returns than high-quality bonds (though with more risk).

In my view, *low inflation and relatively low interest rates will be sustained for a prolonged period as potential growth slows with the decline in the growth of the labour force in Canada, the United States, Europe, and Japan.* On the flip side, developing world growth will continue at a very rapid pace.

Economic Incentives to Reverse the Baby Bust

As fertility rates fall in the developed world and the population ages, dozens of countries have introduced or increased economic incentives for their citizens to have children. These initiatives have been largely at the request of private business confronted with a shortage of young talent, as well as governments hoping to seed their coffers with additional tax money down the road. The coming burden of boomer pensions and health care is weighing heavy on the public and private sector. A meaningful rise in birth rates would augment the workforce of the future, helping to defray these costs.

Since early 2006, fertility incentives have been enacted in at least 16 countries as diverse as Taiwan and Bulgaria. They include baby bonuses, extended paid maternity leave, and tax breaks. Historical evidence does not clearly show how successful such incentives really are. From 1988 to 1997, Quebec had baby bonuses that increased with each additional child, but fertility rates, having plunged since the late 1950s, generally remained very low. Elsewhere, such efforts have been more fruitful.

With the support of Chancellor Angela Merkel, the German government passed reforms to the system of paid parental leave in 2006 to make it economically easier for couples to have children. Germany has an alarmingly low fertility rate of 1.36 children per woman, well below the 2.1 rate needed to maintain the level of the population. The new measures pay parents 67 percent of their salaries, with a ceiling of €18,000, or about US$24,000, for a 12-month parental leave for babies born in 2007 and beyond. A similar incentive was introduced a number of years ago in the the Scandinavian countries and is credited for raising their fertility rate to just over 1.7 despite the very high participation rate of women in the labour force.

Italy, Spain, and Greece lament fertility rates that are even lower than that of Germany. The Eastern European countries that became members of the EU in 2004 have fertility rates that are lower still. Many projects have been introduced to increase the number of newborn citizens, but no significant progress has yet been reported.

Canada, with a fertility rate of 1.5, extended its leave policy to up to 52 weeks (17 weeks of maternity leave and 35 weeks of parental leave), with income support of 55 percent of earnings, up to $413 per week from the federal Employment Insurance program. In fact, if each Canadian parent of a newborn took the maximum leave allowed *at separate times,* the baby would have a parent at home for 89 consecutive weeks (17 weeks of maternity leave plus 35 weeks of parental leave for the birth mother, and 37 weeks of parental leave for the other parent).[5]

The government of Australia credits its 2004 baby bonus with raising its fertility rate from 1.76 to 1.82. France's fertility rate has increased steadily through ever-more-generous tax exemptions for parents with children, and now boasts a fertility rate of 1.9, much higher than that of the EU as a whole.

Japan, on the other hand, experienced only declining fertility rates to a post–Second World War low of 1.25, despite repeated extensions of maternity leaves and other incentives. But very recently there have been some signs of hope. As Japan's fertility rate hit a low of 1.25 in 2005, people there feared the extinction of the Japanese race—now 120 million strong. But Japan has reported that the number of births unexpectedly rose in the first half of 2006, the first increase in six years. With marriages also up over that period, the betting is that births in 2007 might exceed the year before, at last.

The Growing Labour Shortage

Sustaining economic growth in the developed world at what has been a long-term potential rate of roughly 3 percent will be very difficult over coming decades as labour-force growth slows. A country's *potential growth rate* is the combined growth rates of the labour force and productivity (output per unit of labour). It is the rate of expansion at which unemployment rates trend neither higher nor lower, and inflation remains stable at low levels. In global terms, it is hard to overstate the significance of recent U.S. productivity developments. The technology-fuelled acceleration in U.S. productivity growth starting in the mid-1990s trans-formed economists' and policy-makers' understanding of how fast a mature industrialized economy could grow and helped power an American consumption boom that was instrumental in lifting millions out of poverty in export-oriented economies, above all in Asia.

But productivity growth in the United States has slowed as the economy has bumped up against full capacity. This, along with falling growth in the labour supply, portends serious economic deceleration unless steps are taken to mitigate these developments. While many suggested in the late 1990s that the potential growth rate of the U.S. economy might be as high as 3.5 percent because of the surge in productivity growth, today it is generally assumed that, were the economy to grow by more than, say, 3 percent, inflation pressures would mount. Even that figure might be too high, as the Federal Reserve ponders the appropriate economic growth and commensurate level of interest rates that are warranted for a non-inflationary fully employed economy.

Economists at the Bank of Canada have lowered their estimate of potential growth for the Canadian economy to 2.8 percent as productivity growth continues to significantly underperform. For example, between 2000 and 2005, labour productivity improved by 15.5 percent per year in China, compared with an average increase in real wage rates of 13.2 percent. Over the same period, Canadian labour managed a mere 1.7 percent average annual rise in productivity, and average real wage rates barely changed. In the United States, productivity growth, at an average annual rate of around 3.6 percent, well surpassed that of Canada but still did not hold a candle to the surge in China. Typically, poorer countries experience very rapid productivity growth as they move up the development scale; once the economy becomes more mature, productivity growth slows considerably.

The higher the productivity growth of an economy, the higher the wage growth can be without triggering inflation or reducing corporate profitability. *Productivity growth is, therefore, an essential component of rising living standards.* For example, if output per hour rises at an annual rate of 3 percent, the average inflation-adjusted wage can triple over 40 years, so the more that Canadian business can produce for each hour worked, the wealthier the average Canadian becomes. Largely because of the productivity gap, Canadian living standards began falling relative to the United States in 1980. With the rise in the Canadian dollar beginning in 2002 and the commodity boom of the past five years or so, living standards have once again been rising—but they would rise much faster if Canadian business and government were to invest in the technology and training necessary to become more competitive.

This requires more than just will; it also requires the appropriate corporate tax policies and dividend taxation to encourage investment. The elimination of regulatory impediments, foreign investment restrictions, and the freeing of trade between provinces would also help boost Canadian efficiency. Regulatory

approval processes are slow and cumbersome due to the dupli-
cation of work by the federal, provincial, and municipal
governments. As well, governments must allow uncompetitive
businesses to close, something provincial governments are reluctant to do—especially in the Quebec forest products sector, for
example. Tax and competition policy should also be amended to
support investment by larger companies where economies of scale
are important, which would help Canadian companies be more
competitive with large-scale global players.[6] These concerns are
compounded by the rapid slowdown in the growth of Canada's
population in general, and its labour force in particular.

According to Professor Jack Mintz at the University of
Toronto, "Canada has the sixth highest effective tax rate on
capital investment among 36 industrialized and leading developing countries, as well as the eighth highest effective tax rate on
capital when a further 45 developing countries are included in the
comparison."[7] He recommends a reduction in federal corporate
income tax rates, broadened corporate depreciation allowances,
and the elimination of all provincial capital taxes and sales taxes
on the purchases of intermediate and capital goods by business.

Improving productivity growth requires greater savings
flowing into greater investment in technology, capital equipment,
and human capital. This suggests increasing the limits on contributions to pension and RRSP plans and raising the maximum age
for contributions from 71 to 73.[8] Investments in human capital
could be augmented by increases in tuition fee and education tax
credits.

Low fertility rates in most OECD (Organization for Economic
Co-operation and Development) countries and booming populations in poorer nations are eliciting a flood of poor immigrants
into wealthy countries, either through intentionally open doors

or through illegal routes. Private business, facing current or prospective labour shortages, is encouraging governments to relax immigration restrictions. South Korea, which has a fertility rate of only 1.1, is blaming its decline in manufacturing activity on a worker shortage. It reported a 26 percent drop in new manufacturing startups in June 2006 compared to a year earlier.

U.S. hospitals are recruiting nurses from South Africa and Jamaica, and Japan's Sony Corporation recently called for more immigration. In 2004, German company ZDH urged the government to promote the immigration of skilled workers—despite the dilution of the domestic culture from an influx of foreigners that countries such as Germany and Japan have historically feared.

Anti-immigration laws in many parts of the world that were enacted in the decade following the collapse of the Soviet Union in 1991—which opened the floodgates of Eastern European refugees—are now easing. Singapore, Greece, and Finland have reduced their immigration restrictions in response to declining populations. Britain is actively recruiting Poles and other well-educated former-Soviet-bloc residents. Israel has benefited from a massive influx of Russian and other Eastern European Jews, many of whom are highly educated, among them mathematicians, programmers, engineers, physicians, and scientists. Israel boasts the world's highest number of academic publications and university degrees per 1,000 inhabitants.

Recognizing the growing labour shortage, Canada's human resources minister, Monte Solberg, urged boomers in early 2007 to work past retirement age. *Boomers represent about 45 percent of Canada's labour force,* roughly half of them aged 50 and above. The minister urged that Canada should encourage under-represented groups such as the disabled and Aboriginals to enter the workforce, as well as rely to some degree on immigration. He cited a recent PricewaterhouseCoopers business survey that found more than 60 percent of Canadian companies in 2006 felt a shortage of skilled workers was slowing their growth, including 75 percent of businesses in Alberta and 71 percent in Quebec.[9]

Ontario is the fourth jurisdiction in Canada to banish mandatory retirement. The fact that it has done so signals how far the mainstream of public policy has moved since 1990, when the Supreme Court of Canada said mandatory retirement at 65 was "acceptable discrimination." It's also recognition of how boomers are changing the landscape. Discrimination is hard to justify, particularly when the ranks of older people with able minds and bodies are growing and Canada is facing a labour shortage. Ontario's 1.5 million seniors now comprise about 13 percent of the population, but by 2031 there will be 3.7 million people over 65.

Critics worry, however, that this is just the beginning of a shift toward raising the age at which retirement benefits will be paid, forcing many to stay on the job against their wishes. Even supporters of the end to mandatory retirement are critical of the federal government's decision to allow employers to stop benefit payments and pension contributions at 65 for employees who remain on the job.

Quebec and Manitoba eliminated mandatory retirement 25 years ago, and neither province has seen any harm done to pension plans. Indeed, Quebec reduced the pensionable age to 60, a move that was copied by the Canada Pension Plan (CPP). But this all happened before the large boomer generation was approaching retirement age. Unions will undoubtedly try to bargain for the continuation of benefits beginning at age 65. Just as assuredly, however, many cash-strapped employers will try to save money by increasing the age at which pensions become available, hoping that younger workers don't notice or care.

The CPP is well funded and shouldn't have to raise its eligibility age. But the experience in other countries that have ended mandatory retirement is noteworthy. In the United States, the age at which maximum social security benefits can be received is gradually moving to 67. Germany also plans to raise the age for maximum benefits to 67, and in 2006 the British government served notice that by 2046 it intends to increase the state pension age to 68. These three countries, however, face seriously underfunded state pension plans, and aggressive action to raise premiums and reduce benefits is long overdue, albeit very unpopular. We were prescient in Canada to redesign our CPP system in 1997 so that it is now in sound financial shape.

The coming labour shortage will slow the growth of all developed economies, as we have already seen in many parts of Europe and in Japan. It is possible to mitigate or even reverse this slowdown by introducing policies to attract skilled immigrants, increase labour-force participation rates, and increase the productivity of existing workers through training and investments in technology, and by tapping into the rapidly growing labour forces of emerging economies through additional outsourcing. No single measure will be sufficient to reverse the shortage. Most particularly, analysis for Canada shows that even if immigration were to rise to the federal government's announced target of 1 percent of the population—very high by OECD standards—up from the already high proportion of 0.8 percent today, it would not appreciably change the age structure of the Canadian population.[10] Far more effective would be a rise in the average age of retirement from 61 today to closer to 70, which arguably is the demographic equivalent of retiring at age 65 in 1970, given the intervening rise in longevity and the average age of workforce entry.[11]

Ireland is a model of fiscal policy adjustment that reversed a slide in labour-force growth and declining economic status. A country that suffered from net out-migration for decades, and a resulting underperforming economy, Ireland cut corporate income tax rates in 1998 from 32 percent (typical of many industrial countries) to 10 percent, the lowest rate by far in Europe and in any G8 country. Admittedly, this was relatively easy to do, as foreign direct investment in Ireland was low prior to 1998 and the country was correspondingly less dependent on the revenues it had gained at the higher tax rates. But the impact was stunning, and a similar, though less aggressive, lowering of corporate tax rates in Canada would no doubt boost investment and productivity growth here as well.

Ireland quickly won many investment projects by the largest high-tech corporations in the world. Financial and non-financial corporations flocked to the tax haven. The tax cut gave Ireland such an advantage over its EU partners that the European Commission pressured the country to raise the rate to 12.5 percent by 2003. However, those multinationals that had set up in Ireland on the understanding that the 10 percent tax rate would apply until 2010 were allowed to keep their promised entitlements. A flood of Irish émigrés returned home, and people from all over the world moved in as business boomed in the wake of the policy change. Ireland has since been one of the growth leaders of Europe.

People Working Longer

Industrialized countries must do what they can to improve labour-force potential. An important component of that will be older workers. According to Statistics Canada (Statscan), the trend toward working later in life is already evident.[12] For men aged 55 to 74, labour-force participation dropped from 1992 to 1998, reflecting the recession of the early nineties, ageism, business restructuring, downsizing, and forced early retirement. Women were not as negatively affected, but older women were not paid as much as their male counterparts and were not as large a proportion of the workforce. Since that time, older-worker representation in the job market has increased to a new high for both men and women (Chart 16).

In the United States and Canada, the fastest-growing age group in the labour force from 2000 to 2010 will be 55 to 64 year olds, and the second fastest will be the group that is 65 and older (Chart 17). In direct contrast, the number of workers between the ages of 35 and 44 will actually decline in this decade, while

Chart 16

Older Workers: Rapid Labour Force Growth
Participation Rates (% of population ages 55 & over)

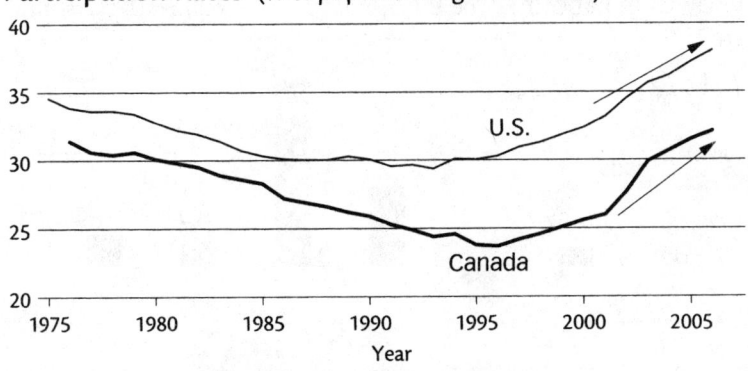

More 55 and Over Working

Sources: Statistics Canada, U.S. Bureau of Labor Statistics.

the 25- to 34-year-old workforce will grow at only an 8 percent pace in the United States and a much smaller 4.8 percent rate in Canada.[13] Canadian business is already concerned about the coming talent war.

A 2006 Conference Board of Canada survey of major organizations found that the most critical near-term shortage will be in leadership and management, as most of these jobs are now filled with people in the "retirement corridor"—aged 50 and above.[14] There will also be a shortage of skilled labour, particularly in fields requiring technical and highly specialized expertise, as the knowledge intensification of work continues.

This is not a deterrent to working longer; it is actually an encouragement. Recent studies show that a surprising array of mental functions hold up well into old age, while others actually improve.[15] For example, vocabulary gets better for those who

Chart 17

The Greying of the Workforce
Growth in Labour Force by Age Group — 2000-10 (% change)

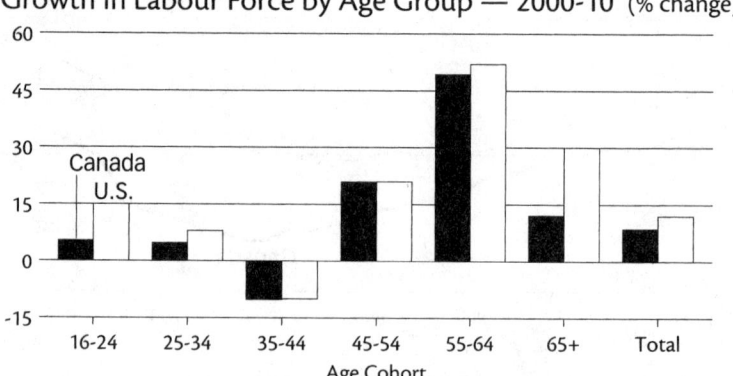

Sources: Social and Economic Dimensions of an Aging Population, McMaster University, Bureau of Labor Statistics.

continue to read, as do other verbal abilities, such as facility with synonyms and antonyms. Older brains are packed with more expert knowledge—information relevant to one's occupation or personal interests. They also store more "cognitive templates," or mental outlines, of generic problems and solutions that can be tapped when confronting new problems.

It has been shown that 60-something air traffic controllers are better and more efficient at keeping simulated planes safely apart than are their 30-something counterparts. Currently, air traffic controllers must retire at 55, but that is now under reconsideration. Older controllers have learned from experience, and are able unconsciously to use that experience to react more efficiently to crisis situations. While the older brain might not be as good at crunching long, laborious calculations, or remembering details, the fact is most often it doesn't need to.

I might have more difficulty today remembering all of the minutiae of the last few months' economic data releases than I did when I was 30, but I've learned over the years that much of that minutiae is just noise, and not in fact worth remembering. My "gut feel" regarding whether a number is important or not is far better than it was in the early years of my career, and experience has taught me how to interpret the data, as well as the more subtle, but important, nuances of policy statements and consumer and business psychology. These are things you cannot learn in school; they come only from years of experience. That is why grey-haired physicians are often far better diagnosticians than young interns fresh out of medical school. Yes, older people forget little things and may have occasional lapses in attention, but their cognitive patterns are so rich they can more than hold their own. Their brains can keep up, even with a diminished supply of blood and oxygen. Put simply, the older worker is experienced enough to separate quickly the wheat from the chaff. Often, young workers don't know the difference between the wheat and the chaff; they waste their energies focusing unnecessarily on the irrelevant or trivial. As a result, the job often gets done better and faster by the older employee.

A growing number of business and public sector organizations are beginning to wake up to this reality and are seriously developing incentives for workers to stay on the job. They must also engage in succession planning and top-talent grooming. The excess demand for labour will shift the job market from an employer's market to an employee's market. Talented job seekers will ponder multiple job offers and salaries will be bid upward. This is already happening in Alberta and other parts of western Canada, reflected in the decline in the national unemployment rate to a generation low. Business, in response, must take action to encourage employee engagement and loyalty by keeping current talent motivated and performing at optimal levels.

Programs to source and nurture top talent are essential to competitive advantage in a world where talent is scarce. *Boomers will want new challenges, flexibility, and compensation that reflect their long dedicated service.* Younger workers want not only challenge but also balance in their life, with family-friendly policies. They want stimulating, varied work, with opportunities to think and act outside the box. Young talent will chafe against bureaucracy and inflexibility at large corporations, which, if they do not change, will rapidly be surpassed by innovative, flexible companies with empowered talent. Boomers' successors will not wait decades to take on serious responsibility and demanding work. They are the action-oriented computer and internet kids that expect instantaneous everything. Many 20-somethings have already started their own successful businesses. They crave independence and will work for big business or big government only if that spirit of independence can be stimulated.

Hierarchical structures will change to more team-oriented activity, where the leader in one project may not be the leader in another. Pay structures must also adjust to this non-pyramidal organization. Many workers will wish to freelance, providing services to many businesses and organizations. This gives flexibility not only to the employee but to the employer as well.

Business and government will also need to create and enhance strategies to retain older workers and to lure back talent that might have left the geographical area in search of better job opportunities. For example, Saskatchewan, whose population is the oldest in Canada, has started a major campaign to lure émigrés back home. Some older industrial cities in the United States, such as Buffalo, New York, are doing the same thing.

Labour-force growth rates will halve in Canada over the next decade, from an annual rate of 1.4 percent today to a mere 0.7 percent by around 2011, and to 0.02 percent in 2021 (Chart 18). The fertility rate in Canada has been below the U.S. rate since 1979. The last published Canadian census (2006) revealed one of the smallest population growth rates on record. While immigration is still a positive factor, accounting for roughly 250,000 new Canadian residents each year, it has not been big enough to offset the low fertility rates of native or naturalized Canadians.[15] Hence, the labour shortage will be more serious here than in the United States, and the need for boomers to stay on the job will grow. This is serendipitous, as many boomers wish to work longer; the incidence of phased-in retirement has nearly doubled in the past five years.

The median age of the *core workforce* in Canada (defined as workers aged 20 to 64) is 42, similar to that in the United States.

Chart 18

Labour Force Growth
(average annual compound growth : %)

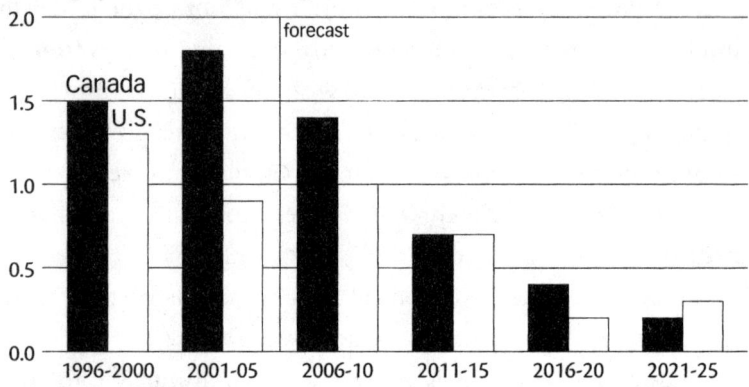

Sources: Conference Board of Canada, Statistics Canada, U.S. Bureau of Labor Statistics.

In the Conference Board study cited above, half the senior executives at the surveyed organizations, and 40 percent of middle management, will be eligible to retire in the next five years. The median age of retirement in Canada has been on a downward trend and is now at 61. Wealth is a major consideration in the retirement decision, thus those filling the highest echelons of organizations are most likely to retire, at least from their current position. Many large corporations in the United States, Europe, and Canada have had a mandatory retirement age of usually 65, but that is quickly disappearing, as it has in government, as the labour shortage and need for continuity and experience becomes crucial.

Paul Hodge, chairperson of the Global Generations Policy Institute at Harvard University, estimates that by 2011, when the first boomers turn 65, the millions of jobs that need to be filled in the United States will outnumber available workers.[17] The gap will be even more dramatic in Canada. We are quickly seeing the demise of programs to encourage early retirement, so prevalent following the tech wreck in 2000. By 2030, the skilled-labour shortage in the United States may be as high as 35 million workers. Over the past 20 years, there has been a 44 percent increase in 25- to 54-year-old workers in the United States. For the next 20 years, no growth in this age group is anticipated, so further reliance on an older workforce, immigration, outsourcing, and productivity growth is essential if economic activity is to remain strong. Clearly, those who feel threatened by outsourcing and immigration (legal or otherwise) are unaware of this reality.

Boomers may well work longer or will view retirement as a gradual transitional process—a period of regeneration. Boomers historically have been low savers. Many boomers look to the equity in their homes for their retirement security. Very few have made realistic plans to replace the income they will lose when they stop working. Moreover, boomers are the healthiest generation of pre-retirees in history. There is good reason to believe that they will not only need to work longer, but they will also want to work longer as they remain quite capable and in need of challenges well into their 70s or beyond.

Labour shortages have already begun in North America, even before boomers have started leaving the workforce en masse. Reports suggest that the university and grad school classes of '07 encountered a spectacular job market, even better than the graduating class the year before. Despite all of the concern about outsourcing—the loss of manufacturing jobs to China and service-sector jobs to India—labour shortages are mounting in accounting, law, construction, trucking, engineering, technology, and even skilled manufacturing, to name just a few.

KEY POINTS

- The U.S. and Canadian populations are aging, but not as rapidly as in other advanced countries. The ratio between seniors and the population is lower than in the rest of the developed world.

- Most developing countries have far younger populations, higher fertility rates, and more rapid population growth than do developed countries; the major exception is China with its one-child policy.

- Dependency ratios are high in the developed world because of the rapid growth in the number of elderly relative to the working population. They are high in the developing world because of the relatively rapid growth in the number of children.

- Labour shortages will mount in the developed world as aging boomers leave the workforce.

- Potential growth in advanced economies will slow unless the decline in the growth of the labour force can be offset by rising productivity growth, increased immigration of skilled workers, additional outsourcing, and later retirement for boomers.

- Productivity growth is essential to raising living standards. We need more appropriate corporate tax policies to encourage investment to boost productivity.

- Businesses and government will adopt policies and pension reforms to encourage boomers to postpone their full retirement from work. This is already happening, and many boomers want and need to work longer.

- Older workers have higher productivity and deal with problems more effectively than younger workers.

Chapter 5

The Aging Population—
What It Means to You

With far fewer workers supporting a rapidly growing number of retirees, all the G8 countries have a looming public pension and health-care problem. In both Canada and the United States, the fastest-growing age cohort between now and 2021 will be those age 65 and older. Over that period, the number of seniors is expected to grow 59 percent in Canada and 51 percent in the United States, compared to overall population growth of a mere 12.5 percent in Canada and a more robust 13.3 percent in the United States. In Canada, this works out to a compound annual-average total population growth rate of only 0.8 percent between now and 2021, down 20 percent from the 1 percent annual growth rate of the past five years. For the United States, the average-annual population growth rate is forecast to be 0.9 percent, slightly weaker than the 1 percent rate over the past five years.

The forecasted population growth in Canada is as close as it is to that of the United States, despite the lower fertility rates here, because it has been boosted by a proportionately larger net immigration gain. Total cumulative immigration as a percent of the population change from 2000 to 2005 was 73 percent in Canada versus only 40 percent in the United States. The real percentage for the United States may in fact be higher, as illegal entry is a huge factor in that country and is not accurately reflected in census statistics. According to the latest census figures, immigrants have continued to surge into metropolitan New York since 2000. That increase, combined with higher birth rates among immigrant groups, has elevated the foreign-born and their children in New York City to 60 percent of the population. The number of people who identified themselves as Mexicans, legally in the United States or not, soared 36 percent in five years.

In 2000, the over-65 population was 12.6 percent of the Canadian total, just a bit higher than the 12.4 percent share in the United States. In 2005, the Canadian ratio was 13 percent, compared to 12.3 percent stateside. By 2026, the ratio will rise to 21.2 percent in Canada, compared to 18.5 percent in the United States, and will continue growing through 2050 to a 25.6 percent share in Canada and 20.3 percent in the United States. While the elderly will comprise a growing percentage of the population in both countries, the rise will be slower south of the border because of the higher American fertility rate. The United Nations suggests that between 2000 and 2025, seniors 65 and over will account for 58 percent of all population growth in Canada, compared with only 25 percent from 1975 to 2000.[1] In the United States, this group will account for a smaller proportion of population growth through 2025: 39.8 percent, still more than double the 18.8 percent rate from 1975 to 2000. On the other hand, the younger generation, those 24 and under, will actually shrink in Canada, reducing population growth by 2.1 percent. In stunning contrast, due to the higher fertility rate in the United States, the 24-and-under cohort there will *grow* 16.3 percent.

In both countries, the aging population reflects the drop in the fertility rate after the baby-boom high and rising life expectancy. But this is not a temporary phenomenon. If fertility rates remain close to current levels and life expectancies continue to rise, as demographers generally expect, the U.S. and Canadian populations will continue to grow older, even after the boomer generation has passed from the scene.

The Canadian Government Pension Plan—Well Funded, but Not So Generous

The Canadian Pension Plan (CPP) is in sound financial shape following significant reforms in the late 1990s. Starting in 1997, contribution rates were increased significantly to build up a large asset base that could generate investment income to help offset potential contribution shortfalls in later years. Even so, CPP premiums are much lower than government pension premiums in the United States.

As well, the CPP Investment Board (CPPIB) was created to enhance returns by allocating a portion of the funds to equity markets, real estate, private equity, and other higher-returning assets. As of June 30, 2006, just over 58 percent of CPP assets were invested in a large number of public or private Canadian and foreign equities, roughly 25.7 percent in government bonds, 5 percent in infrastructure spending including real estate, and 1.2 percent in cash or equivalents.[2] There are significant investments in infrastructure assets such as gas and electricity supply networks, and in transportation operations such as toll roads, bridges, and tunnels. These types of investments usually bring stable long-term real returns. To further outpace inflation, a portion of the bond portfolio is in real return bonds, which move with the rate of inflation. Investments from the CPP have returned an average 8.6 percent annually in the past five years, and the chief actuary expects the total portfolio to grow by 4.2 percent above inflation annually over the long term. Private-sector accountants confirm that this is a realistic goal—the envy of entitlements administrators in the U.S. social security system, as I will discuss below.

Benefits were also tightened slightly in the late nineties, and continue to grow in line with changes in the consumer price index. Quebec runs a parallel pension plan (QPP), which is almost identical in terms of contribution and benefit rates.

The CPP is a model to the world. The development of the CPPIB has made a great difference, as the money in the fund is now invested in a diversified portfolio of assets, allowing for much higher rates of return than were realized when it was invested only in federal and provincial government bonds.

Funding

Investment returns for the plan have been so high that the CPP had assets of $98.6 billion in 2006, more than three times the annual benefits paid in fiscal year 2005. The stock of assets is expected to nearly double by 2013 and will continue to grow until 2022, when it should reach 5.6 times the level of annual benefits paid.[3] After that point, benefits paid will begin to exceed contributions, although the gap will likely be plugged by investment income on the stock of assets.

Contributions to the CPP are from employee and employer, split evenly, totalling 9.9 percent of income. The maximum level of earnings subject to CPP contributions for 2007 was $43,700, with the first $3,500 exempt. Thus, the maximum contribution for CPP is 9.9 percent of $40,200, split evenly between employer and employee, which equals $1,989.90 each (or $3,980 total).

The latest actuarial report on the CPP (2003) found that the sustainable or "steady-state" contribution rate is 9.8 percent, just a shade below the current 9.9 percent level.[4] The report also examines low- and high-side estimates of various assumptions, such as fertility, immigration, and mortality rates, as well as the employment-to-population ratio and market returns; under different scenarios, the range of steady-state contribution rates is between 9.3 percent and 10.3 percent. A more recent report from the federal government's chief actuary says the plan is sustainable for at least 75 years and the fund is expected to grow to $147 billion by the end of 2010.

The other main planks of Canada's public pension system, the Old Age Security (OAS) and the Guaranteed Income Supplement (GIS) for low-income seniors, are funded entirely from general government revenues.

Benefits

One of the main reasons Canada's pension system is well funded is that benefits are modest compared with those in the United States, and they are indexed to the consumer price index (CPI), not wages and salaries as in the United States (Table 2). The maximum benefit paid by the CPP in 2007 to a retiree at age 65 was $10,365 (or $863.75 per month). If he or she begins collecting at age 60, the rate is reduced to $596 per month, and inversely the rate is enhanced to about $1,225 per month if you wait until age 70 to collect—another reason for boomers who feel confident in their longevity to extend their working life. This is a reduction of 6 percent per year for those who retire before age 65

Table 2

CPP/Social Security Comparison

(2007)	Canada	United States
Benefits (annual)		
CPP/Social Security	C$10,365**	US$25,392
Total (US$)*	US$9,013	US$25,392
Premiums (annual)		
CPP/Social Security (combined)	9.9%	12.4%
Max. Earnings	C$40,200	US$97,500
Max. Contribution	C$3,980	US$12,090
Max. Contribution (US$)	US$3,461	US$12,090
Ratio: Max. Benefits/Max. Premiums	2.60	2.10

* (1.15 C$/US$)

** This benefit is supplemented by Old Age Security ($5,903), which starts getting "clawed back" for total incomes over $63,511. For lower income Canadians, there are additional supplementary benefit programs (e.g., Guaranteed Income Supplement). All of these supplementary programs are paid out of general revenue.

to a minimum age of 60, and an increase of 6 percent per year for retirement after age 65 to a maximum of age 70.

An estimated $23.6 billion in CPP benefits and $7.6 billion in QPP benefits were paid in 2004/05, totalling $31.2 billion, or about 2.3 percent of GDP. The intention of the CPP is to replace an average of only 25 percent of pre-retirement employment income, up to the yearly maximum pensionable amount, $43,700 in 2007.

Old Age Security is available to all Canadians over 65, and its payment was $5,903 annually (or $491.93 per month) as of the end of 2006. However, as total income begins to exceed $63,511, these benefits are gradually clawed back, and fade to zero as income reaches $102,865.

At the lower end of the income scale, there are supplements on top of the OAS, most notably the GIS. The GIS pays up to

$7,450.92 (or $620.91 per month), although it is no longer paid for incomes above $35,712. Total government payments of OAS and GIS are estimated at $28.6 billion for 2004/05, just slightly below CPP benefits (and just over 2.1 percent of GDP).

The U.S. Social Security and Medicare System—Seriously Underfunded

Alan Greenspan, former chairman of the Federal Reserve Board, has repeatedly cautioned that a financial shock wave triggered by millions of retiring boomers threatens to turn America's social democracy on its ear and create a society where fewer workers labour under a heavy tax burden to finance retirement programs for the vast number of elderly boomers. Greenspan long ago chaired a committee to study the Social Security system, and despite his efforts then, the system remains woefully underfunded. Social Security is a pay-as-you-go system financed by two premiums levied as payroll taxes paid equally by employers and employees: Old-Age and Survivors Insurance (OASI) and Disability Insurance (DI). They are at a combined rate of 12.4 percent (compared to 9.9 percent for CPP) and applied to a maximum of US$97,500 of earnings (well above the C$43,700 maximum in Canada).

U.S. Medicare is a partial pay-as-you-go system financed by two premiums. The first is Hospital Insurance (HI), a payroll tax paid equally by employer and employee with no maximum. The other is Supplementary Medical Insurance (SMI), a monthly premium (US$88.50) paid by beneficiaries. This monthly premium is nowhere near enough to finance the SMI; the bulk of the SMI program is funded by federal general revenues. *Medicare is an even bigger concern than Social Security,* as it has been growing at a 6.7 percent annual rate since 1995 and is expected to accelerate to a 9 percent annual rate over the next decade.[5] It is projected to reach 11 percent of GDP by 2081, compared to 3.1 percent in 2006. In contrast, over the same period, Social Security is expected to rise to 6.3 percent of GDP versus 4.2 percent in 2006.

Much of the problem has been the sharp rise in the length of retirement. When Social Security was passed in 1935, the average retirement age was 69. That age fell to 67 by 1950 and to 62 in 2006. In 2003, for the first time, more Americans chose the reduced Social Security benefits at age 62 rather than waiting for the full benefit that started at 65. Surveys suggest that until recently, despite improving health, Americans, Canadians, and Europeans mainly wanted to retire earlier, not later.[6]

Many estimate that Social Security trust fund assets will be exhausted by 2041, and the system will be able to fund only

Table 3

U.S. Trust Funds—Key Dates

	OASI	DI	OASDI	HI
First year outgo exceeds income excluding interest	2018	2005	2017	2006
First year outgo exceeds income including interest	2028	2013	2027	2010
Year trust fund assets are exhausted	2042	2026	2041	2019

Source: Trustees of the Social Security and Medicare Trust Funds, 2007 Annual Reports.

74 percent of its generous scheduled benefits (Table 3). For 2007, the maximum Social Security benefit was US$25,392. This compares to a much smaller C$10,365 maximum CPP benefit, which is supplemented by an OAS benefit of C$5,903. (The OAS payment begins to be clawed back for retired Canadians with total income of more than C$63,511.)

The American OASI program could be brought into actuarial balance by immediately increasing premiums by 16 percent or by immediately cutting benefits by 13 percent, or some combination of the two, neither of which is politically palatable. One change that *has* been made is that the age at which maximum Social Security benefits will be paid is gradually rising from 65 years now for those born in 1937 and earlier, to age 67 for those born in 1960 and later. A bill to further increase the retirement age to 68 was introduced in 2005 by Republican senator Chuck Hagel but did not become law.[7] Washington is aware that it must continue to increase the age for full Social Security retirement benefits to help take some pressure off the system.

The Medicare HI trust fund assets will be exhausted even sooner, by 2019. In 2006, benefits paid by HI exceeded income *excluding* interest. In 2010, HI benefits paid will exceed income *including* interest. It can be brought into actuarial balance by immediately increasing premiums by a whopping 121 percent— an HI combined employer/employee payroll tax of 6.41 percent instead of 2.9 percent—or by immediately slashing benefits by 48 percent, or a mix of the two.

Needless to say, this is a political time bomb. Despite President Bush's emphasis during the 2004 election campaign on fixing the Social Security and Medicare systems, he was unable to convince Congress to do anything, even when he had a Republican majority in both houses. Social Security was hotly debated, but there has been little mention of the HI program, because everyone is afraid to touch it. It is as sanctified as the Statue of Liberty. The system is clearly in dire straits. With the bulk of all health-care expenditures occurring in the last two years of life, the Medicare bill will rise astronomically as the population ages and health-care costs per beneficiary continue to rise.

Projections of future medical costs are fraught with uncertainty, but history suggests that without significant changes in policy these costs are likely to continue to rise more quickly than incomes, at least for the foreseeable future. Together with the aging of the population, ongoing increases in medical costs will lead to a rapid expansion of Medicare and Medicaid (the federal-state health-care program for low-income earners) expenditures in the United States and the federally funded public health-care system in Canada.

As big a burden as Social Security is for the United States, it represented only 4.3 percent of GDP in 2004 and is slated to rise to about 6.3 percent in 2050 (excluding Medicare). The numbers are far higher in many other countries. For example, public pension plans in the Euro zone as a percentage of GDP were 11.5 percent in 2004 and are forecast to rise to 14.1 percent in 2050.[8] Sweden took steps as long ago as 1999 to address this burden by tying pension benefits to salaries, life expectancy, and the health of the economy. It is still too early to assess the system, as a full generation of retirees have yet to be affected, but Poland, Brazil, and Russia have adopted elements of the Swedish plan and others are studying it.

Essentially, what the plan does is require Swedes to contribute 18.5 percent of their salaries to the pension system, of which 2.5 percentage points are held in individual accounts. Each year, workers are sent statements showing what they have put into their pension and what they would get at retirement. Individual payouts fluctuate positively with salary and economic growth, and negatively with life-expectancy rates. This gives people incentives to be more productive, thereby earning more money, and to retire later. The official retirement age in Sweden is 61, but since the new pension plan kicked in, the average age has risen to 63.

European labour unions are unlikely to approve such a plan in the traditional social-welfare countries of core Europe. From a macroeconomic perspective, the plan has its drawbacks. For one, it increases income inequality in old age, whereas Social Security and the CPP help to even out income distribution. As well, a slowdown in economic activity would reduce pensions, acting as an automatic destabilizer and contributing further to the economic slowdown. The jury is still out on this system, but it does lend flexibility to accommodate revenue and demographic shifts.

The Elderly versus the Rest

Currently, people 65 years and older make up just over 12 percent of the U.S. population, and for every one of these people there are about five between the ages of 20 and 64. According to the intermediate projections of the Social Security Trustees, the ratio between the two age groups will have fallen from the current 5:1 to 3:1 in 2030, as the elderly share of the U.S. population rises to 19 percent.[9]

The developed economies are entering a time when fewer workers will be supporting a rapidly growing number of retirees. In the United States from 2001 to 2030, federal revenues as a percentage of GDP will remain roughly steady, while Social Security, Medicare, and Medicaid's share of GDP will just about double.[10] If the increased cost of these programs is to be paid with tax hikes, the Social Security/Medicare tax would need to increase to a combined rate of 30 percent from 15.3 percent today. We can only imagine the resistance this would generate from employers and employees as "age warfare" ensues. We see a taste of that in Florida today, where the elderly represent about 18 percent of the population. Workers urge the government for better schools and highways, while seniors demand caps on property tax rate increases and better medical care.

In the coming years in the United States, elderly programs may take up to two-thirds and more of federal revenues, according to the expert testimony of Paul Hodge, director of the Harvard Generations Policy Program, at the 2005 White House Conference on Aging.[11] That would force non-elderly programs—including such essential expenditures as defence, agriculture, law enforcement, and interest payments on the national debt—to shrink by more than half. Hodge asserts that "though it is politically difficult, there are graduated, equitable solutions to these challenges."

The U.S. federal Centers for Medicare and Medicaid Services estimate that health-care spending will double in the next decade to US$4.1 trillion, or nearly 20 percent of the general economy. The Medicare drug benefit introduced in 2006 increased the U.S. government's share of health-care spending from 28 percent in 2005 to 39 percent the following year. Medicare's spending alone (which now includes drug coverage for low-income Medicaid enrollees) was up 22 percent in just that one year, as Medicaid spending was flat. Many now believe that with the aging population, the current U.S. public-private health system will eventually be primarily a public-health system, and at some point Medicare will be the largest piece of it.[12]

Canada faces similar issues. According to Statscan, by 2012, half of Canada's workforce will be 55 or older; close to a quarter of them will be over 60. Greying Canadians have legitimate worries about the rising cost of health care and the eroding funding base for the social safety net. As stated in a recent C.D. Howe Institute study, "The implicit liabilities from health care are the biggest long-term challenge facing Canadian governments ... with the provinces bearing its brunt. Declines in the share of GDP devoted to education and child benefits provide partial offsets, but the total net demographically driven liability of more than $810 billion rivals the funded debt of all levels of government and the unfunded liabilities of the C/QPP."[13]

The prospect of growing fiscal imbalances and their economic consequences also raises essential questions of intergenerational fairness. Future generations will bear a growing burden of the debt generated by underfunded government medical programs and experience slower growth in per-capita incomes than would otherwise have been the case. Over time, we must move toward fiscal policies that are sustainable, efficient, and equitable across generations. In both the United States and Canada, we need to develop intergenerational strategies and to minimize the political rhetoric and encourage collegial bipartisan problem solving. Policies are required to increase private and public savings, enhance productivity, encourage the immigration of young talent, and make the workplace as accommodating to older workers as possible.

Developing Economies Help Pay the Price

In recent years, the United States stepped up its support for the poor in emerging countries. The approval by the U.S. Food and

Drug Administration of a new once-a-day pill against AIDS could at least contribute to health in developing countries. The news follows approval earlier in 2006 of a cervical cancer vaccine, which may save more than 200,000 lives each year in poor nations.

In the United States, these breakthroughs have coincided with unprecedented political support for the funding that pays for such medicines. In 2005, the House of Representatives passed its foreign aid bill with 393 votes, the highest tally in more than two decades. Over the past six years, the United States has increased six-fold the money it spends to fight scourges such as AIDS and tuberculosis abroad.

But the heights America has reached in such spending may represent the peak of foreign aid, leaving only a large decline ahead. As the funding required for Social Security and Medicare skyrockets, something else in the budget will have to make way—and America's foreign aid program is one of the likeliest candidates for cuts.

Twenty years ago, Social Security, Medicare, and Medicaid—to name only the three largest U.S. entitlement programs—made up less than 30 percent of the nation's budget. Today, they take up 40 percent, and in another 10 years they are projected to constitute fully half of all spending.

As entitlements have grown in the past two decades, the share of America's economy going to foreign aid has been halved. Even the share devoted to national defence has declined by more than 40 percent. The unsustainable promises made by successive governments, primarily to older Americans, could hobble U.S. foreign policy for decades.

With 3 billion people around the world still living on less than two dollars a day, the inability of the United States to offer support in the future will have huge geopolitical implications. Clearly, the world's view of the United States depends on the gap between income per capita there, now more than US$43,000 a year, and income per capita in the poorer regions of the world. The growth in the aged population will burden the United States with even larger budget constraints. For the rest of the G8— particularly Europe, Russia, and Japan—the constraint will be even greater, creating the conditions for a potential slide in the improvement made to date in narrowing the economic and health gap between have and have-not countries.

KEY POINTS

- Large numbers of retirees will strain the pension and health-care systems in most industrial countries.

- The Canada Pension Plan (CPP) is well funded and is considered to be a model to the world, as its assets are more than three times the benefits paid in 2005 and assets are expected to double over the next decade.

- The above stands in stark contract to the U.S. Social Security and Medicare systems, which are seriously underfunded. Medicare—the U.S. health-care system for the elderly—in particular is a huge concern and is considered to be a political time bomb.

- CPP is, however, far less generous than Social Security. In today's dollars, maximum annual CPP payments are only C$10,365, which could be supplemented by a C$5,903 Old Age Security (OAS) benefit. (The OAS payment begins to be clawed back for retired Canadians with total income of over C$63,511.) In contrast, the maximum annual Social Security benefit for 2007 was US$25,392 (over C$28,000, assuming a Canadian dollar just shy of US90¢).

- Boomers with average working income beyond median levels could not maintain living standards on CPP alone.

- Funding requirements for Social Security and Medicare will come at the expense of other government spending programs.

- Canada, too, faces enormous increases in the cost of providing health care to an aging population. We will struggle to keep up with the latest in technology and medical advances, particularly under the burden of the rising incidence of chronic disease.

- All boomers are faced with the prospect of some private spending on health care as they age, as well as the considerable burden of long-term care either at home or in a nursing home.

- Governments will be torn between the needs of boomers (health care, pensions, safety, public services) and those of young families (schools, highways, affordable housing, daycare). There could be significant conflict between age groups. This requires immediate action and planning.

Chapter 6

Lifestyle and Health Planning

The goal is a healthy, active, secure retirement that will last for as long as possible. But to achieve it, planning is essential. While most consider retirement planning to be solely a financial exercise, a successful retirement takes more than just financial forethought. As I discussed earlier, lifestyle and health planning should also begin years before retirement, and it is an essential component in determining the appropriate financial plan. You cannot know how much income you will need in retirement if you don't know where you might live and how you would choose to spend your time. And, of course, your health will determine the length of your retirement and your ability to travel and live an active, independent life.

The best way to approach retirement planning is first to develop a lifestyle plan. It might be more difficult than you think, especially if you have a partner with different tastes. One of you likes adventure travel, while the other likes reading on a beach. One might prefer Florida, while the other is hankering to live in Maine. Be it a ski resort or a warm-weather locale, one home or two, condo or a single-family dwelling, rental or ownership, a quiet university town or the hustle and bustle of a city—these things need to be considered and at least tentatively decided. Trying out different possibilities before retirement would inform the decision. There are many resources to help you assess what you could do next—your strengths and talents, the activities you would find enriching and gratifying. If you have a partner, or children and grandchildren, their views are important.

Once this aspect of your retirement is sketched out, you will be better able to create a provisional budget and thereby determine the income you will need when you finally stop working or cut back on your workload.

For many households, retirement income needs might be well below pre-retirement levels once work-related expenses and saving for retirement are finished with. Expenses could be cut further by downsizing your residence or by moving to a less expensive area. But for others, income requirements might rise, as travel becomes a larger element of your budget, for example, or as new pastimes or hobbies begin to necessitate large capital and maintenance expenditures, such as living half the year in Palm Beach, or buying a boat or even an RV. While later in retirement people tend to slow down and spend less money, long-term care, either at home or in a nursing home, can be extremely expensive. In addition, finding space in an assisted-living centre is getting tougher, with waiting lists and soaring prices placing added burdens on consumers shopping for a property.

It is also important to determine how much of your retirement income requirements will be covered by government (CPP or Social Security) and employee pensions, and how much you will finance from your own nest egg. Then it is fairly straightforward to calculate just how big that nest egg needs to be the day you stop working.

Humans Are Purpose-Driven

For people who define themselves by their jobs and have few outside interests or non-business social contacts, retirement planning is especially important. Often, those who started their own business and ran it for years have trouble letting go, even if a daughter or son is taking over. Many entrepreneurs never actually retire; they just pull back and eventually slow down.

If you define yourself by your business card and look mainly to your job for the respect and attention we all need, leaving work can be traumatic, especially if the decision was not entirely yours. In the early 2000s, after the stock market crashed, many businesses restructured, laying off thousands of workers. Often the higher-paid 50-something workers were the first to go, and at that time no one was hiring grey hair. Fortunately, as the labour shortage becomes more and more evident, senior talent is increasingly valued once again. Many look forward to a less hectic and stressful lifestyle but then find in retirement that having too much time on their hands is disconcerting and in its own way stressful. A gradual reduction in working hours might be best for these folks, giving them time to redefine themselves and develop other interests, get involved in volunteer work, join corporate boards, or take up other rewarding activities.

It is very important to have a purpose in life that is meaningful to you. It lends structure to your day, keeps your mind active, and provides social contact and a sense of accomplishment. Even people in the most horrific circumstances have attributed their mental and physical survival to the fact that they maintained a sense of purpose and accomplishment.

Especially late in life, it is important to keep your mind active and your days full. We all know of people who died prematurely soon after they retired. It's probably better for most to ease into retirement. Stay on the job, if possible, later than traditional retirement age. Slow down your work pace gradually over a few years. Continue this way as long as you still gain satisfaction, mental or physical, from your work. It not only helps financially, it makes a meaningful difference to your well-being.

Working during the early-retirement period markedly reduces the amount of money you need to sock away before you stop working full time. For example, someone who requires $50,000 in annual retirement income from age 65 to 90 would have to accumulate a nest egg of about $704,700. This would require annual savings of $5,834 starting at age 25 (assuming a 5 percent real rate of return). However, by gradually phasing in retirement, and working just enough through the age of 70 to cover expenditures with after-tax income, the required nest egg shrinks to about $450,900 (Charts 19 and 20). This requires a

Chart 19

Transitional Retirement Eases the Burden

Savings (thousands of Cdn. dollars)

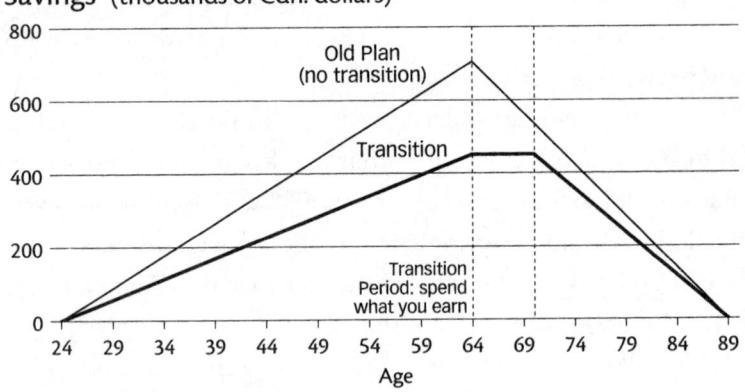

Source: BMO Financial Group.

Chart 20

Work During Early Retirement Reduces Savings Needs

Savings Needed at Age 65 (thousands of Cdn. dollars)

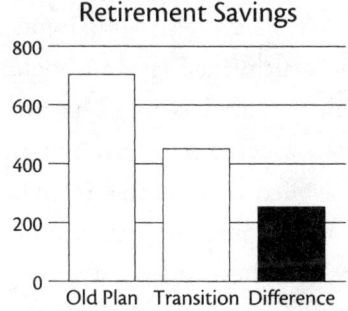

Retirement Savings

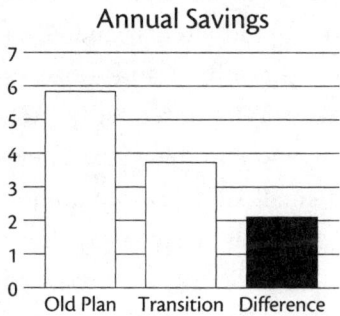

Annual Savings

Source: BMO Financial Group.

more manageable $3,733 in annual savings, or just 64 percent of the savings needed if there is no transition period.[1] Many enjoy the intellectual stimulation, human contact, and, of course, money associated with part-time or flex-time work. Surveys suggest that more and more boomers are intending to work in retirement. The financial benefits of this trend are clear, and with the labour shortage the benefits go to both employer and employee.

How Do You Know When It's Time to Stop Working?

The whole concept of retirement is relatively new. It was only in the past two generations—those of boomer parents and grandparents—that people expected to live much beyond the day they stopped working, because they stopped working only when they physically had to. Not only did people have too little money to retire prior to the introduction of government pension plans, but life expectancy was shorter than the government's minimum legal retirement age. My great-grandparents were still working when they passed away—as were my paternal grandparents, and my father. My maternal grandparents, on the other hand—cushioned by healthy savings and Social Security—retired early. Actually, they retired twice. The first time was in their 50s. They sold their grocery business, bought a small single-storey home, and travelled the country in their car. They were away for about three months, driving the United States from coast to coast, and they had a ball. Then they visited Hawaii—a dream of theirs—followed by Cuba, where my grandfather had lived for two years as an immigrant teenager before he entered the United States.

Once all of that travel was finished, they realized they were bored. They bought another grocery store and went back to work for ten more years. It wasn't until my grandmother was diagnosed with terminal cancer at age 65, when Pop was 70, that they actually retired for good. My grandfather went on to live on his own, quite actively and independently, until he was nearly 90. When he, too, was diagnosed with incurable cancer, he refused treatment, said good-bye to all of us, and died quietly in his own bed less than a month later. I've always aspired to have that much control over my life.

I suspect it was the advent of Social Security and CPP and their rules for full benefits at 65 that created the mindset to retire by age 65 even if you are capable of working. People say, "Take the money early, at 62 or younger, and enjoy life. Do your travelling while you're healthy. Let somebody younger deal with the stress at the office." But today, with life expectancy so high, boomers might consider delaying full retirement. If we wait until age 70, we get even bigger cheques.

It's tempting to think about Freedom 55, especially when I haven't had enough sleep or I'm not feeling well. But I know that retirement is not just about money or turning off my alarm clock. As a major step in life's journey, retirement is momentous, and it deserves careful consideration.

I think it is helpful to organize your thoughts according to a checklist of pertinent factors, from health to wealth. Here is an outline of what to consider.

Your Health

The state of your health has a huge impact on your retirement decision. If it has been a real physical effort to drag yourself to work every day, by all means get the rest and care you need. If work will damage your health further, retire as soon as you can financially do so. Clearly, people with chronic medical problems or life-threatening illnesses should consider their health first.

If you are still healthy, however, you should think the decision through in two ways. Retiring soon would give you what are presumably the healthiest years you have left for your own enjoyment. But on the other side, you might not want to check out when you are still healthy and raring to go. Why not work a few more years and sock more money away for a cushier, more secure retirement? You can always retire if you find your job satisfaction waning. Remember, this is a personal decision. Even mates have different views on retirement and do not necessarily retire at the same time or the same age.

Your Job

How much you like your job is another major factor in making your retirement decision. According to a U.S. Gallup Poll in August 2005, 87 percent of working adults in the private sector "love" or "like" their jobs.[2] A not-insignificant 12 percent "dislike" or "hate" their jobs. And interestingly, another Gallup Poll, in June 2006, found that 33 percent of working adults are very or somewhat concerned about "losing a sense of purpose" in their lives after they retire.[3] There is a trend toward a longer working life, and we see that in Canadian surveys as well.

Even if you decide to retire from your current career, you can consider starting a new one. This is the time you could reinvent yourself in your own business, a new job, or a portfolio of activities, some paying and some not. You might be interested in teaching or mentoring. If you have a particular passion or hobby, consider the viability of turning it into a business. There are many great sources available to help you think creatively about this; outplacement firms and a whole host of books counsel people over 50 about career transition.[4]

Work can be more flexible than ever before. The internet, cellphones, and video conferencing allow you to work from almost anywhere, and it is only going to get easier with new technologies. Most employers will face talent shortages and will be so keen for your skills and expertise that you can call the shots, working as much or as little as you want.

Your Plans

With the right financial planning, retirement can be a time to fulfill your dreams and follow through on plans you never had time for before. These could include travelling, developing new hobbies or pursuing old ones, moving to a different locale, learning a language, building your dream home, taking courses, writing a novel, perfecting your golf swing, spending more quality time with your grandchildren and friends—there is no limit to the possibilities.

Determining your location is a very important step; it will help determine how much money you will need when you stop working, and what your options could be for part-time work. You might want to split your time between two (or more) locations. For many Canadians, a warmer climate in the winter is attractive. Just remember that you must be in the country for six months each year to maintain your residency and qualify for Canadian health care. If you do want to leave permanently, remember to consider the departure tax and the cost of health insurance elsewhere. These are big decisions and should be made in consultation with appropriate tax accounting, legal, and financial experts who have experience in dealing with these issues in Canada and in your desired location. If you plan to move to a new location, local experts there should also be consulted. It is wise to live in this new place at least a few weeks at a time, and at different times of the year, before you take the plunge. And wherever you live, make sure there is easy access to good health care and that your residence will still be appropriate if you become less fit and nimble. Security is a concern as well. Older people are vulnerable, so you want to live in a place where you feel safe.

It is also important to consider your partner, if you have one, as well as family and friends. Some people find it exciting to move to a new locale—but just make sure the place is welcoming to newcomers. Others would miss family and friends too much to move away permanently. Sometimes friends will relocate together, at least for part of the year. Being near to children and

grandchildren is wonderful, but remember, they could go wherever their careers or education take them. If your decision is based
solely on them, you might one day find yourself standing in the
way of their mobility.

Your Wealth

The biggest hurdle to clear for retirement is financial, although
many people won't admit it. Assess how much risk and uncertainty you can handle; what seems sufficient for one person might
cause sleepless nights for another with the same standard of
living. Consider longevity risk, market risk, currency risk, and
contingency risk. Some people are extremely risk averse, and
others are more laid back. Know what feels right to you.

A 2006 U.S. Gallup Poll found 60 percent of Americans are
very or moderately worried about funding their retirement.[5] Just
50 percent of working adults in the United States say they expect
to have enough money to live comfortably, down from 59 percent
five years earlier. Survey evidence in Canada is mixed, but to me
the U.S. numbers appear a bit higher than they would be for
Canada, as more people here still have defined-benefit pension
plans. But for many people who don't work for large corporations, or work outside the public sector, the defined-contribution
RRSP is their only private sector pension, and CPP is far less
generous than Social Security in the United States.

A separate U.S. poll, also conducted in spring 2006, found
that 60 percent of those who expressed little or no concern about
their retirement finances said they would likely work in retirement.[6] An impressive 71 percent of non-retired adults with post-
graduate education said they would likely work in retirement,
compared with 64 percent of those with some college education

and 60 percent of those with none. What this suggests, a Gallup analyst wrote, is that "a major cultural realignment is under way concerning the way Americans view retirement." Our surveys of Canadians yield similar conclusions.

KEY POINTS

- The goal for most boomers is a long-lasting, healthy, happy, active, and secure retirement. That might sound like a pipe dream, but I'm convinced it is achievable with the right long-term planning and preparation. Certainly, we all will be hit with the unexpected; preparing to deal with it is part of the process.

- Develop a lifestyle plan for retirement. It will help determine (and be determined by) how much income you will likely need (and have) in retirement. Develop this plan long before retirement and test it out. You might be surprised; what you thought was ideal may not be so. With a partner, this becomes a joint decision, and that in itself is challenging.

- Consider what too much togetherness might mean. Maybe a place large enough for each of you to have your own space would be a good idea.

- Retirement could well be a very long period of time. You might want to think of it in stages: the first decade, the second decade, and so on. Or base the stages on your health and ability to live independently.

- There is no need to rush into retirement; consider all the issues very carefully. Most people will want to phase it in—working fewer hours, but still working.

- Similarly, don't rush into location decisions. Test a place first by living there for at least a few weeks at a time, and during different times of the year. You might consider renting before you buy.

- If you are toying with the idea of leaving Canada permanently, get expert advice and think it over carefully. There are serious financial and health-care ramifications.

- Consider your friends and family as well before moving.

- Your health is paramount. Do what is best for your health and well-being. Even if you don't have sufficient money to live big, it is possible to find great contentment in a small town, for instance, where the cost of living is markedly lower. But make sure you have easy access to good health care.

Chapter 7

Dollars and Sense

How financially prepared are you for the day you stop working? Figuring out the answer to this question is a fundamental step in preparing for the new retirement. While there is a rapidly growing number of millionaires in Canada and the United States, it will take millions of dollars for many people without traditional pensions to maintain their living standards during retirement; the more affluent you are, the more money you will need. What matters most is the value of your investible funds, such as stocks, bonds, and cash—not so much your illiquid durable assets, such as homes, cars, and boats. Homes, of course, can be sold or mortgaged, if necessary, but most people wouldn't want to rely on that. In this chapter we will look at how much in investible assets you need the day you stop working.

Household wealth in Canada is higher today as a proportion of after-tax income than virtually ever before, as asset values have risen sharply. For example, homeowner equity has risen sharply and now represents one of the largest components of household net worth. Most boomers, however, do not expect the equity in their homes to finance their retirement.[1] Most report that they would prefer to stay in their homes and would not consider a reverse mortgage, where the bank pays you a monthly annuity for a portion of the equity value of your home and then takes owner-ship of the house upon your death.

Nearly 70 percent of all households in both Canada and the United States own their own home—an historical high. For this reason, debt as a percent of disposable income has also hit record highs, as a home mortgage is generally the largest component of debt for most households (Chart 21). Debt-servicing costs have escalated with the rise in debt and any uptick in mortgage rates, and "active" savings rates have fallen sharply in both countries. *Active* saving is defined as income minus consumer spending; *passive* saving includes a rise in unrealized capital gains on your assets and employer contributions to your retirement plan. In the

Chart 21

Household Finances a Concern

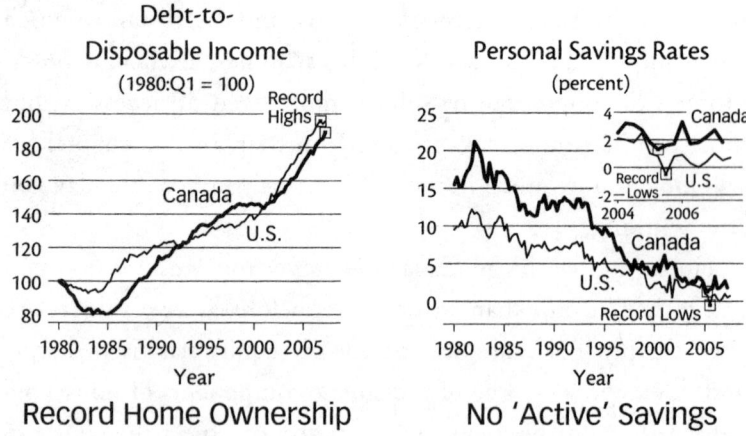

Sources: Bank of Canada, Statistics Canada, Federal Reserve Board, BEA.

United States, the aggregate household active savings rate turned negative briefly in 2005.

Low savings rates are particularly troubling in the United States, where, in the aggregate, Americans are spending more than they earn, financed by the surge in mortgage-equity withdrawals through mortgage refinancing and home-equity loans. Homeowner-equity extraction slowed in 2006, however, as interest rates increased and the housing market weakened, taking house prices down. A more muted decline in savings rates has occurred in Canada as well; savings rates have fallen sharply, but still remain positive. Consumers don't seem to feel the need to step up savings in either country, because wealth continues to rise, as passive savings balances continue to increase.

Half of U.S. families and about a third of Canadian families with heads of household over 65 have debt, but the value of that debt relative to net worth is not excessive. Debt relative to net worth has increased sharply in the last decade in both the United States and Canada as more households have become homeowners. But this has occurred mainly in the under-45 age group, people who still have their peak earning years ahead of them to prepare for retirement. Retirement awareness is rising, as the percentage of families with retirement accounts, and the median value of those accounts, has trended upward over the past decade.

Even with the surge in debt and the fall in active savings, household net worth—defined as assets minus debt and other liabilities—has risen to historically high levels in North America, owing mostly to the surge in house prices and the recovery in the value of pensions. But the housing market slowed dramatically in the United States in 2006, far faster than during any of the postwar recessions. The median house price nationwide fell for the first time since the Depression, and residential construction activity came to a near standstill. Sales of new and existing homes fell sharply. Homebuilders felt the pinch, especially in the luxury market. The pace of house-price decline varied across the United States, with the biggest losses in the formerly hottest markets, mainly on the two coasts and in Las Vegas. Florida was particularly hard hit. In the middle of the country, most house prices were stable or up very modestly in 2006.

Household net worth is now 5.7 times disposable income in the United States, which is well above the long-term average of 4.8 times, but below the peak posted during the stock-market tech bubble in 2000 (Chart 22). During that time, American households held more of their wealth in equities than in any other asset class. Today, pension values and homeowner equity are the largest components of wealth (Chart 23).

Chart 22

Wealth Rises
Net Worth (% of personal disposable income)

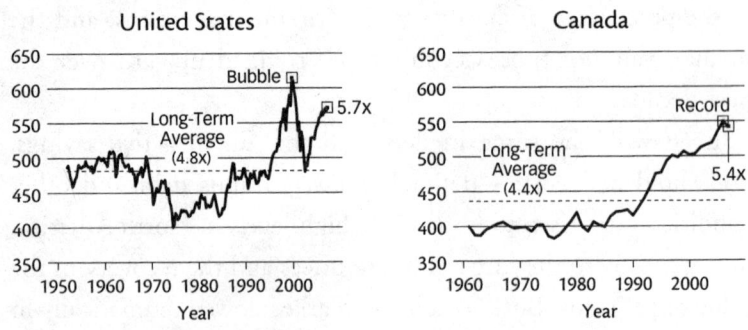

(Assets – Debt) / Personal Disposable Income

Sources: Statistics Canada, U.S. Federal Reserve Board.

Chart 23

All Wealth Gains on Paper
Household Assets ($ trillions outstanding)

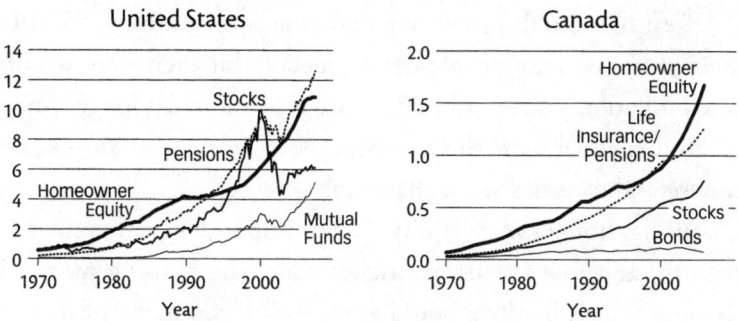

Homeowner Equity Dominates

Sources: Statistics Canada, Federal Reserve Board.

Household net worth in Canada is at a near record level relative to disposable income, as Canadians were not quite as exuberant about stocks in the late nineties. Here, the wealth ratio is 5.4 times disposable income, and the composition of wealth is similar to the composition in the United States, but as housing markets remain strong in Canada homeowner equity now takes the lead.

In both countries, however, average wealth-to-income figures are misleading because income and wealth distribution has become so skewed, with the top 10 percent of income earners owning a disproportionate share of the wealth. While the gap between rich and poor has widened, that gap remains bigger in the United States than in Canada. That is why the *median* wealth-to-income ratio—at 3.5 in Canada and 2.3 in the United States—is so much lower than the average aggregate levels. The *median* is a statistical middle, above which and below which

50 percent of the values lie—in this case, 50 percent of the household wealth-to-income ratios. Because so few families have so much wealth, the average (or mean) ratio is biased upward and is much higher than the median ratio.

Wealth is also disproportionately concentrated in the 55-to-64 age group, because people don't generally hit their peak wealth-accumulation years until their youngest child is no longer financially dependent on them, when the bills start to shrink and household earnings are at their peak.

While homeowner equity is an important component of wealth, and most of us feel richer when the housing market is booming, it is hardly a liquid asset. And if too many of us were to tap this source of wealth by selling our homes and downsizing, the price of homes would plummet and equity would decline. Older boomers might not make out so badly if there were only a trickle of sellers. But should we decide en masse to put our homes on the market, to whom would we sell? And at what price?

As I described earlier, the real retirement nest egg is investible funds—money in retirement accounts or non-registered accounts that is invested in assets that are relatively easy to sell when needed, such as stocks, bonds, cash, and other financial instruments. Funds in retirement accounts are non-taxable until money is withdrawn, while realized capital gains, dividends, or interest income in non-registered accounts are taxable. In exchange for the tax deductibility of contributions to retirement accounts and their tax-free growth, withdrawals are fully taxable at ordinary income tax rates; for most people, income tax rates are higher than the tax rates on dividends or realized capital gains earned in non-registered accounts. However, interest earned is taxable at ordinary income tax rates.

The Widening Income and Wealth Gap

Never before has the gap between the "haves" and "have nots" been so wide, nor the haves had so much.[2] Wealthy boomers are, in general, far more affluent than their retired parents, but in the United States especially, the wealth is highly concentrated among a relatively small segment of the coming boomer gerontocracy. New research from the University of Michigan's Retirement Research Center finds that the median total net worth of early boomers is just US$151,500.[3] Subtract housing and any illiquid business assets, and this figure drops to a paltry US$48,000. For the top 10 percent, however, the figures are US$888,000 net worth and roughly US$537,000 excluding illiquid assets. For the top 5 percent, the numbers are US$1,327,000 and US$903,600, respectively. The distribution of wealth and income in Canada is not quite as skewed, owing to a more progressive tax system and generally lower incomes at the very top 1 percent, but it is a far cry from being evenly distributed. It is likely that many older boomers will be better off than younger ones, having got into the thriving housing, stock, and jobs markets earlier.

This concentration of wealth is giving the world's affluent a greater capacity than ever before to spend and invest. Most noteworthy, the return on education has never been higher. That is why Ben Bernanke, chairman of the United States Federal Reserve Board, recommends that the labour dislocations caused by technology and globalization be addressed with improved access to education and training. Government should enhance U.S. labour mobility by making health and pension benefits more portable and offering retraining and job-search assistance to displaced workers.

Many in Canada and the United States have benefited immensely from the asset boom—including investment bankers, commodity traders, oil executives and investors, merger lawyers, hedge-fund impresarios, senior management, and art dealers—and this helps explain why broad consumption figures defy the pessimists—recessionists and "perma-bears"—who argue that the plunge in the U.S. housing market or the rise in mortgage foreclosures for subprime borrowers will cause a sustained and meaningful slowdown in economic activity in the United States and, therefore, Canada. But by far the bulk of spending, tax revenues, and assets in the economy is attributable to the wealthiest 20 percent of the population.

Those of lesser means in the developed economies are suffering or stagnating financially by comparison, though in absolute terms standards of living are holding up or advancing modestly. This is the nexus of the expanding "wealth gap" that some lament, others celebrate, and all debate. A long-term pattern in which the rich continue to get rapidly richer seems durable.

For years, both the number of wealthy households and their aggregate resources have been growing much faster than the global economy. A 2006 Capgemini-Merrill Lynch *World Wealth Report* estimates that the number of people globally with financial assets exceeding $1 million climbed 6.5 percent in 2005, and their combined financial wealth rose 8.5 percent, to $33.3 trillion.[4] Many of these high net worth individuals (HNWIs) have financial assets of many millions, even billions, of dollars. No longer does being a "millionaire" mean being particularly rich. Million-dollar homes are common in many large cities; the median price of a home in Vancouver, for example, is over half a million dollars. The highest growth in HNWI populations in 2005 was South Korea, India, Russia, and South Africa, but from a very small base.

In the United States, according to the liberal think tank the Economic Policy Institute, the richest 1 percent of Americans had net wealth 190 times that of the median household, up from a ratio of 168 in 1998 and 131 in 1983.[5] The top 1 percent owned 37 percent of all domestic stocks held by individuals in 2004, and the top 10 percent owned 79 percent of all stock held by individuals. The real income of the richest 5 percent of U.S. residents climbed an aggregate 31 percent from 1985 through 2004, versus 14 percent for the middle 20 percent, and 12 percent for the bottom 20 percent.

The top 20 percent of wealth holders in the United States owned 65.4 percent of total housing equity in 2004, while the bottom 80 percent held just 34.6 percent (one benefit of which is that most of the household equity is in stable hands with virtually no risk of delinquency or foreclosure). Even more dramatic, the bottom 80 percent in wealth class held just 7.9 percent of stock excluding pensions, and that share only increased to 9.4 percent when pensions were added. Put the other way, the top 20 percent in wealth owned more than 90 percent of stocks held by individuals and pension funds. This belies the argument that house and stock prices will plunge when the bulk of the boomers retire; *the fear of asset liquidation in retirement makes no sense when most of the assets are in the hands of the wealthiest people, those who won't need to liquidate.* In fact, the wealthiest retirees will be accumulating financial assets as their portfolio incomes exceed their spending. An extensive study by the U.S. Government Accountability Office in July 2006 comes to the same conclusion: the retirement of boomers is unlikely to precipitate a dramatic decline in market returns.[6] Not only is financial-asset ownership highly concentrated among the wealthiest boomers, but also, "as baby boomers gradually enter retirement, the share of the population age 65 and older is projected to continue increasing until about 2040, at which point it is expected to plateau. Thus, the aging of the baby boom generation, in conjunction with the aging of the overall U.S. population, is a cumulative development rather than a sudden change."[7]

As well, large parts of the developed world are awash in liquidity and are investing in U.S.-dollar assets. And Brazil, Russia, India, and China will continue to grow faster than the United States, and as they accumulate wealth, U.S. and Canadian financial markets will benefit.

The wealth distribution is skewed in Canada as well, but not nearly to the same degree it is in the United States. According to Statistics Canada, the top 20 percent of boomer families by wealth class owned 72 percent of all financial assets *excluding* employer and other pension plans, and the top 50 percent owned 92 percent of these financial assets. *Including* employer and other pensions, the top 20 percent by wealth class owned 64 percent of all financial assets, and the top 50 percent again accounted for 92 percent of assets.

There are several factors that explain the widening gap between rich and poor. The income premium on higher education has grown in recent years as the economy has become increasingly service-based, rewarding those with better communication, organizational, and creative skills. Educated parents are passing on educational and economic advantages to their children, while those lacking education have fewer reliable, well-paid manufacturing jobs available to them. This contributes to a "winner-take-most" economy; the middle class in the United States has suffered modest inflation-adjusted declines in household income in recent years.

The opening of the global economy to competitive and capitalist incentives has allowed innovators and developers to access deep global supplies of funding and large global markets for their products and services. The lowering of tax rates on capital gains and dividends in the United States and Canada has also disproportionately benefited the wealthy.

With technology allowing cheap global communication, information and entertainment products can easily reach a vastly larger audience than ever before. Economists have long theorized that technology would help create a class of super-rich celebrities. Brad Pitt is worth what he is because his movies can play to audiences numbering in the billions. Satellite TV has meant that English soccer star David Beckham could go from a team in Manchester to one in Madrid to one in Los Angeles, where he has been given a $250 million five-year contract and will be watched by sports fans in Europe, Africa, Latin America, and North America.

The proportion of U.S. GDP now attributable to corporate profits is near a multi-decade high. These profits are driven by global demand and large productivity gains. They drive strong dividend and capital-gains income toward the affluent, while restraining the wage growth of the middle class.

Globalization's increase in competitive pressures has reduced the number of high-paying manufacturing jobs in both the United States and Canada—jobs that did not require a university degree. This has been compounded by the legacy problems and over-capacity in the American automobile industry and the decline in U.S. residential construction.

Virtually any product that can be mass produced by unskilled labour and shipped is already produced overseas or soon will be. But that still leaves a good deal of manufacturing in North America. For example, high-end goods that are too large or delicate to ship and require skill to produce and service are still manufactured in the United States and Canada. There are physical and strategic limits to globalization. Sensitive electronics or customized products are most efficiently produced near the customer, where installation and service can be more easily handled. These high-value-added products will continue to be manufactured in North America.

The American and Canadian move to service economies was once anticipated to create nations of hamburger flippers and movie-ticket takers. But among America's and Canada's key exports are the investment banker, merger lawyer, corporate board member, and business consultant, travelling to London, Rio, or Shanghai to cut billion-dollar deals.

In the service sector, many very-high-paying jobs cannot be outsourced. Many advisory businesses—including auditing, law, dentistry, much of medicine, market research, financial planning, marketing, real estate sales and development, and so on—require face-to-face contact. Jobs in any business where knowing your customer is important cannot be outsourced. If the job cannot be programmed into a computer, it cannot be explained sufficiently to an absent foreign worker, no matter how skilled. Foreigners cannot replace the synergies and analytical advantages provided by local knowledge and team brain storming. With all the available technology for remote communication, people still prefer dealing in person, with speakers who are live, and doing business with people they know for transactions that require significant expertise or expense. North America and other developed regions continue to have a competitive advantage in high-end service businesses, as well as in local services such as restaurants, hair stylists, and taxis. But the knowledge intensity of the high-end service businesses is rising, so greater rewards will continue to go to those with the greatest intellectual firepower. In most cases, this means a continued inequality of income and wealth distribution.

Common Retirement Risks

Boomers' choices in retirement will differ significantly from those of their parents. Yours will not be your father's or mother's retirement. As we know, boomers are healthier, better educated, and more affluent than their parents were at the same age. They generally have fewer children, and had them later in life. Many boomers have blended families from earlier marriages, which likely suggests that their net worth was split at one point with an ex-partner, putting significant additional risk to retirement security. As well, most boomers have already travelled more than their parents at their age and have a greater yearning for additional travel to more exotic locations, which increases their income needs in retirement. Most boomers will be more active than earlier generations were and continue to engage in sports and fitness activities well into their elder years. They will live longer with fewer disabilities, so they must protect themselves from the risk of running out of money, in other words, from longevity risk.

Your odds of beating the average life-expectancy figures may be higher than you think. The numbers are based on the general population, but if you're reasonably affluent and you've taken care of yourself, you're likely to live longer. Indeed, insurers figure they are dealing with wealthier, healthier people— and assume their clients will live maybe two years longer than the general population.

Longevity Risk

This is the financial nightmare feared by many boomers: outliving your money. There are new ways available to guard against this danger. Your monthly Canada Pension Plan (CPP) or Social Security cheque provides a partial safety net (but only to a maximum in 2007 of a mere C$10,365 a year in Canada and US$25,392 a year in the United States), and you may have further protection from a traditional defined benefit (DB) pension, the old-fashioned kind that pays a percentage of your average maximum salary. This payment is lifelong and often continues for your surviving spouse, albeit at a reduced level. Some boomers are even lucky enough to have a DB plan that rises with the cost of living. Unfortunately, most boomers will not have a DB pension; instead they will have the increasingly prevalent "defined contri- bution" (DC) pension, an RRSP in Canada or a 401(k) in the United States. Contributions to these are generally voluntary, and few people contribute the maximum allowed over their careers, and even that might not be enough for some affluent folks.

While funds contributed to these plans are tax-exempt and grow tax-free, they are fully taxable as income when funds are withdrawn in retirement, even though much of the money might have come from dividends and capital gains that are normally taxed at preferential rates. Moreover, capital losses in a retirement account cannot be used to offset capital gains else- where in your portfolio of assets. At the end of the year of your 71st birthday, it is mandatory that the RRSP be converted to a RRIF (Registered Retirement Income Fund), with withdrawals starting at 4.76 percent of the asset value and increasing with age. In the United States, mandatory withdrawals from the 401(k) begin at age 70 years and six months, with minimum initial withdrawals of approximately 3.6 percent.

Finally, and maybe most importantly, the value of your DC plan depends critically on your investment prowess over your career. Too many people have found themselves too heavily invested in their own company stock or otherwise not sufficiently diversified. Catch a bear market early in your retirement and you could be forced to sell assets at markedly depressed prices. This is why it is no longer considered sensible to assume withdrawal rates of more than 5 percent. But your smartest move may have nothing to do with Bay Street or Wall Street. If you're really worried about outliving your savings, the best thing you can do is to delay starting your government pension plan. Let's say you are 62. Instead of taking CPP today, you could put off benefits until as late as age 70—thus locking up a lifetime stream of inflation-linked income that's 61 percent larger.

Some people will want even more assurance that even if they live to be 105 they will not run out of money. There is now a slew of products available to help protect you in your later years. These are relatively complex products that prudently require the counsel of a financial adviser, as circumstances differ from person to person.

Annuities Options such as annuities and reverse mortgages, both of which have their pluses and minuses, can offer assured income even if you hit your centennial birthday. Aside from CPP or Social Security and a DB pension, annuities are about the only source of guaranteed lifetime income. For seniors, however, the best ones are usually immediate annuities, which begin to pay out within one year of purchase. Annuities are longevity insurance. Generally they are a contract guaranteeing lifetime income— fixed or variable depending on the terms. They can be bought with a single lump-sum premium or with periodic payments over a pre-specified period.

Another wrinkle is longevity insurance that is bought at, say, age 65 in return for income that starts at age 85. Thus you are free to spend your assets over the first 20 years of retirement, knowing you have guaranteed income thereafter.

Annuities have three advantages: (1) they provide lifetime income; (2) fixed annuities guarantee a set amount of income; and (3) the income is partly tax-free because it is seen as a repayment of capital if the annuity is purchased with funds that originated outside a registered plan. Otherwise the full amount is taxable.

Like everything else, however, you pay for the assurance of a certain income. Guarantees cost money, often more than they are truly worth with hindsight. That's what the insurance company actuaries determine. They are betting on actuarial probabilities about your life expectancy and rates of return on investments. The insurers certainly have a margin of safety for themselves built into the premiums. The main drawback is that you could die soon after buying an annuity, not collect much income, and have the bulk of the money end up in the hands of your insurance company rather than your heirs. Other disadvantages of annuities are that they are usually irrevocable; the income, though guaranteed, might not keep up with inflation; and the income is only as good as the solvency of the insurer. Despite these disadvantages, annuities might make sense for some, but they should be considered carefully with an independent professional adviser. Of course, the larger your nest egg the day you stop working, the lower your longevity risk will be.

Reverse Mortgages Reverse mortgages offer an income-generating option for people over the age of 60 who have substantial equity in their home and little other investment money. StatsCan reports that in 2001, 75.4 percent of seniors aged 65 to 74 were living in homes they owned, the bulk of which were mortgage-free. People are apparently reluctant to sell their home, even as they age; for the 75 to 84 age range, 68.4 percent still lived in their own home, and for those 85 and over, 57.8 percent still did so. In those two age categories, most homes are owned mortgage-free.

According to Canada Mortgage and Housing Corporation (CMHC), you can borrow 10 to 40 percent of the appraised value of your house. The younger you are, the lower the proportion of equity you can borrow. This is to help ensure the value of the mortgage never exceeds the future value of your home. You can receive the money as a lump sum or a regular stream of income, or some combination of the two. The income comes from a life income annuity and is therefore tax-sheltered and continues as long as you or your spouse lives in the house. The loan is paid back at death or when you choose to sell.

This is an expensive option. The fees and costs of these loans are higher than they are on regular mortgages. In mid-2007, that was about 8 percent for a variable-rate reverse mortgage and substantially higher for one at a fixed rate. For example, the five-year fixed reverse mortgage rate was a whopping 9.3 percent in mid-2007.

In the United States, reverse mortgages are broadly similar to those in Canada with respect to age restrictions and the amount that can be borrowed. The difference is in the interest rate used and the fees charged. The interest rate in the United States is the one-year Treasury bill rate plus a margin set by the Federal National Mortgage Association (known as "Fannie Mae"). In mid-2007, it was similar to the rates in Canada and well above rates on traditional mortgages. The markup for the monthly adjusted rate is 1.5 percentage points, and 3.1 percentage points for the annually adjusted rate. Also, an annual fee of 0.5 percent of the outstanding loan is tacked on. An interesting twist in the United States is that borrowers must attend pre-loan counselling before they can take out a reverse mortgage.

The people who benefit most from reverse mortgages are those who are house-rich but cash-poor. They are not for people who intend to move soon or who want to leave the full value of their home to their heirs. It is probably advisable to wait as long as you can before getting a reverse mortgage to maximize the value of your potential income and estate. Once again, consult a qualified professional before taking action.

Income Risk

Boomers will also carry more debt into retirement than previous generations did and many could underestimate the level of income they will need to support their desired lifestyle. This is *income risk*. A host of new instruments are now available for investing for income. Investment advisers can walk you through the options, including traditional debt securities (bonds), dividend-paying stocks, preferred shares, income trusts, and closed-end funds. In addition, convertible debentures and equity-linked notes offer a combination of income and the potential for capital appreciation. The main drawback to investing in debt securities is that bond interest is subject to the ordinary income tax rate (as high as roughly 46 percent in Ontario, 35 percent in the United States), which is higher than the tax on dividends (as high as 25 percent in Ontario, 15 percent in the United States) and capital gains (as high as 23 percent in Ontario, 15 percent in the United States). These tax rates vary modestly from province to province. This tax treatment, combined with persistently low interest rates, has caused investors to look for tax-preferred alternatives. The tax issue becomes relevant in non-retirement accounts when the income is earned; it is relevant in registered retirement accounts when the income is withdrawn, although in registered accounts, all withdrawals are taxed at the income tax rate.

As with any investment, individuals should consider their personal circumstances, investment goals, and risk tolerance before making a decision. Your investment adviser can make specific recommendations customized to your needs.

Contingency Risk

Just because you are retired doesn't mean that unexpected expenses don't still pop up occasionally. Your roof might leak or your car might break down, and having a bit of a cushion for these contingencies is sensible.

An important component here is the rising cost of health care and particularly long-term health care. In addition, many boomers will be supporting elderly parents during their own retirement, the cost of which could be extremely high. Long-term-care insurance is one possibility to deal with this risk for their own elder years, which makes sense if you have insufficient retirement assets or wish to leave assets to your heirs.

Wealth Insurance At your death, the fair market value of your RRSP or RRIF is included as income on your final tax return and is subject, in most cases, to the highest marginal tax rate. It can be transferred tax-free to your spouse if he or she is named as beneficiary. This may also apply to dependent children or grandchildren who are the named beneficiaries. But at your surviving spouse's death, any remaining value is fully taxable as income. It is possible to preserve the value of your pre-tax wealth with a tax-free death benefit from life insurance to cover estate settlement costs. This decision, of course, is a personal one and depends on whether you want to leave a sizeable estate, the cost of the premiums, and the adequacy of your retirement income. In some cases, life insurance is cost effective, and your beneficiaries might well offer to pay the premiums.

Estate and insurance advisers hold the keys to making these decisions and should be consulted early enough for you to make plans well in advance of retirement. The same is true of long-term-care insurance, which covers the cost of nursing-home or in-home care up to a maximum amount per day, depending on your policy. This, too, might be seen as wealth insurance, because it increases the chances of your having wealth remaining when you die to leave to your heirs. It is especially valuable if you might not have an estate large enough to cover the cost of this increasingly expensive care. In some cases, the premiums in excess of the payout could be reimbursed to your estate if you have owned the policy for a specified period of time (usually measured in decades). Premiums, however, can be quite high depending on age, health, and family history. But if there is a risk of running out of money, it could be a wise investment, even though it does reduce retirement income and all returns on the premiums invested over time are forfeited.

In the United States, where government health coverage for seniors is more limited and more costly, and where estate taxes can be onerous, long-term-care insurance and life insurance to cover tax bills are more attractive. U.S. estate taxes can take as much as a 46 percent bite out of estate values bequeathed to heirs other than a surviving spouse for estate values above $2 million in 2007 (rising further until 2010, when the tax rate will temporarily fall to 0 percent until current law is changed).

Beware

Unfortunately, there are unscrupulous wolves in sheep's clothing out there. A host of ill-suited financial products—from reverse mortgages to life-settlement contracts and variable annuities—are targeted at retirees. The sales pitches for these products are designed to tap into deep-seated fears about the affordability of retirement. Don't fall for high-pressure tactics, and certainly don't take action until you have discussed it with a trusted family member or financial adviser. In addition, it is prudent to seek legal and tax advice as well.

For example, a life-settlement contract is a financial transaction in which you sell your life-insurance policy for more than the policy's cash value, but less than its face value. The hard sell is that you turn your insurance policy into cash while you're still alive to enjoy it. For people who no longer need insurance but who do need cash, selling an unwanted policy can generate more money than cashing in a policy. The strategy can be particularly appealing with term-life policies, which have no cash value and which policyholders would otherwise let lapse.

The negatives, which they won't tell you, are that if you continue to need insurance coverage, selling an existing policy isn't wise. Rates to replace your coverage could be unaffordable, or you could become uninsurable. Also, you're spending money your heirs may need after your death—and while insurance benefits paid to heirs held in an irrevocable trust for a specified period of time can be income-tax-free in Canada (they are generally tax-free in the United States), the profits from selling a contract are taxable at ordinary income rates, which are generally the highest tax rates. There is no fix for this if you have second thoughts later. Once you sell your policy, you can't get it back.

Inheritance—Not Such a Big Windfall

Surprising to many, an inheritance will not be a significant source of retirement income for most boomers. According to a recent U.S. survey by the American Association of Retired Persons Public Policy Institute (AARP PPI), far fewer boomers have inherited, or will inherit, money than financial services companies suggest.[8] The AARP PPI analyzed the Federal Reserve's Survey of Consumer Finances, which gives cross-sectional household data for 2004 (unfortunately, there are no similar recent data available for Canada) and concluded that baby boomers may have already inherited a significant chunk of the money they're going to receive. A key finding: Just 19 percent of boomers have received an inheritance, and only 15 percent still anticipate one.

As it turns out, it is a lot more expensive for boomer parents to live in old age than many anticipated, especially given the huge cost of long-term care. And they are living longer and therefore spending more. While most medical costs are covered by the government in Canada, long-term care for other than the indigent is only partially covered, in some cases by the provincial government, whether it is at home or in public nursing homes. There is a long waiting list for nursing home beds in much of Canada. Similarly, Medicare does not cover long-term care in the United States until it becomes hospice care.

The AARP PPI study points out that among boomer households that have already inherited money, the typical bequest was US$64,000, figured in 2005 dollars. While 81 percent of boomer households have not received an inheritance and expect relatively little, 7.5 percent have received more than US$100,000. Once estates are split among multiple siblings— and boomer families were large—there isn't much left for any single boomer to rely on.

If these sums are inherited by younger boomers with 20 years or so to go until retirement, they could be the start of a sizeable retirement nest egg, making up for many spending excesses and investment mistakes. But evidence suggests that while most boomers will not inherit a significant amount, even those who do too often mismanage the money. The younger the beneficiary, the more likely the money will be put to ill use. It would be far better to pay down debt, and/or invest the money wisely, consistent with an overall retirement plan.

Not surprisingly, the lower the level of assets, the greater the anxiety and alienation that those surveyed associate with retirement. Fewer than 50 percent of pre-retiree responders said they knew how much money they would need the day they stopped working; moreover, most did not know how much pre- or after-tax income they would need in retirement to maintain their established lifestyle. Most pre-retirees expect to use about 80 percent of their assets to fund their own retirement, compared to 12 percent to support children or grandchildren, 6 percent to build a legacy, and 2 percent to support parents.[9] With so little expected to go to legacy building, boomer kids should expect little in retirement support from inheritance as well. This is certainly consistent with many boomers' lifelong behaviour of spending today and worrying about tomorrow ... tomorrow.

There is a good deal of uncertainty in retirement planning. Given that the length of retirement is unknown, asset bases should likely be bigger than most would expect, but a premature death could create legacies that are much larger than you expected to leave.

Most boomers also expect to have debts in retirement. The traditional view of debt-free living in our senior years has not been passed along by boomer parents. In Canada, most of that debt is expected to be in credit card liabilities or lines of credit. In contrast, Americans are less likely to pay off their mortgages because of the tax deductibility of both mortgage interest and property taxes on their primary residence.

Anecdotal evidence suggests that most boomers do not have a formal retirement plan and that most do not anticipate selling their primary residence. Boomers expect their lifestyle in retirement to remain unchanged, although this might be more of a hope than an expectation. Unlike their parents and grandparents, most boomers expect to hold a meaningful share of their retirement portfolios in equities. The low interest rates of the past decade have influenced this view. Their biggest worries about retiring are serious illness and having insufficient income to maintain their lifestyle.

Heirs?

Timing things so that you die broke is of course very dicey. But even the very wealthy are concerned about leaving too much to their heirs. Warren Buffett, age 76, has said that wealthy parents should leave their children with enough money to do anything they want, but not so much that they are doomed to do nothing at all.[10] Most wealthy Canadians and Americans get rich through their own efforts and unyielding ambition. Many fear that if they leave their children too much, it will rob them of the joys of achieving success. But the line between what is enough and what is too much is blurry, and some children know at a very early age that they will always be wealthy through no toil of their own. Some wealthy parents use their money both as a stick and a carrot, rewarding the children who do what they are told and punishing the ones who do not.

Marlon Brando and Joan Crawford are known to have done this from the grave, cutting some of their children completely out of their will.

And while we are on the subject, make sure you have a will, and see to it that it is kept up-to-date. Nearly half of Canadians die without a will, causing untold estate battles among family members. You might want to give some assets to your heirs before your death, although doing that could trigger a deemed disposal of the asset and therefore capital gains taxes. Some people bequeath the family cottage before their death, but you should consult a tax expert before doing so. Also, naming your spouse as the beneficiary of your retirement accounts allows the money to be passed tax-free. When the surviving spouse dies, the retirement money is then taxed as income in the last year of his or her life. These issues are complicated and often have unintended consequences. Advice from an estate lawyer and an accountant is well worth the price.

Most wealthy parents, regardless of their own frugality, feel the drive to pass on their money to their children. Sam Walton, the founder of Wal-Mart, was known for his thrift, yet he left behind a dynasty that will affect his heirs for generations. His four children are multi-billionaires and come up repeatedly on the list of the richest people in America. Recently, they tied for fourth place behind only Bill Gates, Warren Buffett, and Paul Allen, according to *Forbes* magazine.[11] Some people are more impressed by those who make their money than by those who leverage it. Yet Steven Forbes and Donald Trump, both members of the lucky-sperm club, believe that with the right upbringing, heirs aren't doomed to unproductive or tragic lives (though they'd be unlikely to think otherwise).

Increasing numbers of wealthy individuals and families are setting up charitable foundations—most notably Bill and

Melinda Gates and Warren Buffett. In their case, much of their money is going toward disease treatment and prevention in Africa and other emerging economies. These high-profile donations by billionaires might encourage more of the mega-rich to do the same. Even if only a small proportion of the world's roughly 800 billionaires did so, the impact would be substantial.

Of course most of us cannot give fantastic sums, but we can give our time and expertise. Personal involvement in charitable giving will be important for boomers. We will provide ready assistance in fundraising and charitable projects. With the wisdom of a full life, new time on their hands, and the wealth to finance their lifestyle, boomers will have an unprecedented chance to engage in volunteerism and other acts of philanthropy. Many will want to give back to society and apply their career skills to non-profit endeavours. This will help to bring business talents to the non-profit sector and generous donations of money. In 2004, a study by Statistics Canada found that in the non-profit sector, finding sufficient numbers of skilled volunteers was one of the top two concerns, along with long-term funding.[12] As well, the 2006 change in Canadian tax law to exempt from capital gains taxation all charitable donations of publicly listed securities will encourage a substantial increase in philanthropy. The donors receive the tax credit for charitable giving, so it is a win-win situation.

Boomers will want to take an active role in their favourite charities, assuring their money is well spent. This will encourage better governance and creative new fundraising ideas. Individual and family foundations allow donors to direct money to the causes that are most important to them. Get professional tax advice so this is done in the most tax-effective way, stretching the value of the dollars given. Boomers will want to leave their mark on society. Look for a sharp increase in educational and health-care endowments and donations, gifts to the arts and sciences, and giving to specific needs of the poor. There is a growing number of very effective charities for battered women and indigent women in need of a job. Many will choose to mentor or tutor those who are less privileged.

The growing number of immigrants will create needs for English-language training, and all of the basic necessities. With birth rates relatively high in the immigrant communities of Canada and the United States, this group will be a source of future labour force growth, but often they need a helping hand to better assimilate and deal with the cultural differences in their new home.

KEY POINTS

- For the day you stop working, you may need more money than you think.

- Most important is the value of your investible funds, such as stocks, bonds, and cash, rather than physical assets, such as cars and homes.

- You can, of course, sell your home or take out a reverse mortgage for your retirement, but most people don't want to do that. If too many boomers were to attempt to sell their homes at the same time, prices would drop sharply, so you cannot count on home-owner equity to remain at peak levels.

- Wealth as a percent of household disposable income in Canada has risen to a near-record high, mostly because of the rise in homeowner equity, employer contributions to pensions, and the rate of return on those contributions.

- *Active* savings rates—the proportion of your after-tax earnings you do not spend—have fallen sharply in Canada in recent years and are even lower still in the United States.

- A record of nearly 70 percent of Canadian households own their own home, and mortgages are the largest single component of household debt.

- Paying off your mortgage is an important step to retirement security.

- Wealth is disproportionately concentrated in the 55 to 64 age bracket.

- The inequality of income and wealth distribution is widening in Canada and even more so in the United States. In our knowledge-based economy, education is paramount. Highly educated parents spawn highly educated children, so the gap between rich and poor persists and even widens.

- Large nest eggs are required to cover the uncertainties of not knowing how long you will live (longevity risk), how large financial asset returns and inflation will be (income risk), or how much money you might need for unexpected but necessary expenditures (contingency risk).

- Rely on accredited experts with experience and references to devise your investment plan. Any consideration of financial issues, such as annuities, reverse mortgages, and long-term-care insurance should be discussed with a disinterested expert. There are plenty of unsavoury characters who prey on older folks, and often wipe out their savings.

- Diversification of assets is also essential. We know what happened to retirees who were solely invested in their company's stock when troubles emerged. Think of Nortel retirees who invested in company stock at the peak, not to mention Enron.

- Most people cannot count on spectacular bequests to assure their retirement security. Boomer parents are living longer, the cost of long-term care can quickly swallow up wealth, and the large families of the baby-boom era mean that bequests get split among siblings.

• Boomers will want to give back to society. Volunteerism, donations, and posthumous gifts will become increasingly common as boomers age.

Chapter 8

Have Boomers Saved Enough for Retirement?

While older boomers are concerned about their financial future, most believe they will live well in retirement. They are certainly a more sanguine bunch that their parents, whose outlook was influenced by the travails of the Depression and world war. No one has ever accused the boomer generation of being overly parsimonious, and for some there will certainly be troubles ahead, especially for those in the United States. Savings rates are lower in the United States than they are in Canada, house values have declined there, and the old-fashioned defined benefit pension plan is disappearing fast. Also, retirees in the United States will likely carry a higher debt burden, as mortgage interest is tax deductible, providing less incentive to pay down debt.

Pension Plans

According to a January 2003 Statistics Canada study, roughly 40 percent of paid workers were participating in Registered Retirement Plans (RRPs), which are financed at least in part by employer contributions.[1] Membership in these plans is restricted to paid workers in an employer-employee relationship, so the self-employed with unincorporated businesses, unpaid family workers, and the unemployed are not eligible. There are two kinds of RRPs: defined benefit (DB) and defined contribution (DC).

DB plans are the traditional ones, usually offered by the public sector and banks, insurance companies, and some other large corporations. Under these plans, after 30 to 40 years of work you are guaranteed pre-tax retirement income at levels that are 30 to 70 percent of pre-retirement earnings, depending on the provisions of the particular plan. Under the DB method, benefits are guaranteed and determined by a stipulated formula; employer contributions are not predetermined but are instead calculated on the basis of actuarial valuations taking employee contributions, if any, into consideration. You know you will receive some established annual pension income, usually based on your years of service and your most recent few years of annual compensation, assuming you are not subject to an income cap. Many DB plans have an income cap of, say, $125,000 to $200,000. If your most recent average income was above the cap, you will have to close the gap with your own savings. There is no income (market) risk or longevity risk in your retirement income, and most plans are adjusted for the cost of living to cover inflation risk.

People with these plans are sitting pretty, especially those who have put in their 30 years at a relatively young age. Many military personnel, airline pilots (at least until lately), and teachers, for example, retired with full pensions in their early- to mid-50s and then went on to begin other careers. In addition, organizations providing these plans often pay for benefits as well, such as group life insurance and dental and medical insurance, and these plans often continue after your death at a somewhat reduced level until the death of your surviving spouse. Thus, DB plans are an annuitized flow of monthly income during the whole of your retirement and that of your spouse. You can't do better than that.

Under the DC plan, the employer and employee make contributions, but much of the risk and cost associated with providing an income flow during retirement is shifted from the employer to the employee. Pension benefits depend on the size of accumulated contributions *and* on the return on investment. This is the rub: Even if you have made maximum allowable contributions all along, something most people haven't done, bad investments or a string of bad markets could slash your portfolio value and put retirement security in jeopardy. You really have no idea what your annual retirement income might be until you near the end of your working career, and even then it remains subject to market risk.

In Canada, of the 40 percent of paid workers who were covered by RRPs in 2003, 82 percent were in DB plans. In other words, nearly 33 percent of paid workers in Canada were covered by DB plans. Most DB plan members work in the public sector (Chart 24). Private-sector employees are beginning to question the use of their hard-earned tax dollars to cover the cost of the plush retirement plans of government workers. This questioning is encouraged by the perception that public-sector employees work fewer hours per week and have at least somewhat more job security and benefits.

Since the early nineties, there has been a shift in Canada from DB plans, where the employer takes the risk, to DC plans, where the onus is on the employee. This is especially true in the private sector, but even in the public sector some plans have shifted from DB to DC. A Watson Wyatt study released in 2006 found that

Chart 24

Majority of Defined Benefit Plan Members are Employed in the Public Sector

Canada (millions of members)

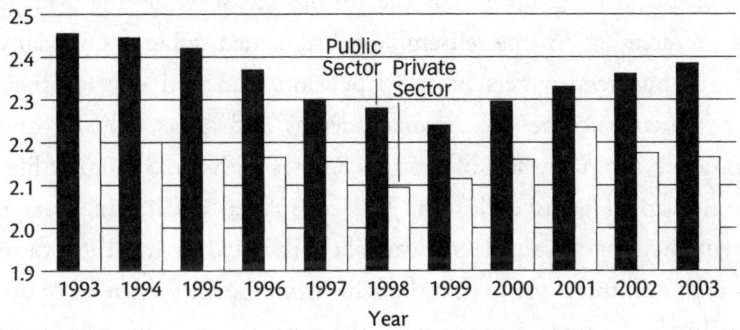

Source: Statistics Canada.

half of chief financial officers in Canada had made, or were planning to make, changes to DB plans, including shifting to DC.[2]

According to a study from the Canadian Federation of Independent Business, Canada is on its way to a two-tier retirement system, where many public-sector workers will be assured of gold-plated, fully indexed pension plans and many private-sector workers will be lucky to have a pension at all.[3] According to the study, underfunded liabilities among public sector pension plans could lead to future tax increases, dragging down the economy, productivity, and prosperity, while the growing gap between public sector plans and less generous private sector plans could lead to greater income and social inequity.

The public sector has driven the early retirement trend that started in the 1980s. Their pensions are so generous, they feel they needn't work to age 65. In 2005, roughly 56 percent of public sector retirees had retired early, compared with 33 percent in the private sector and only 20 percent of the self-employed. The average age of retirement in the Canadian public sector has decreased to 59 from 64 in the mid-1970s, compared with a decrease to 62 from 65 for the private sector, while the average retirement age for the self-employed remained stable at 66. Many small business owners have no pension plan and rely for their retirement income on personal savings and assets, RRSPs, and proceeds from the sale of their businesses with the $500,000 lifetime capital gains exclusion. The substantial decline in average retirement age in the 1990s was likely initiated by the 1987 drop in the minimum age to draw benefits from the CPP from 65 to 60.

In the United States as well, the nation is split in two: those who have government benefits and those who don't. The gap is growing in every way: pensions, medical benefits, and retirement ages.[4] Retired government workers are twice as likely to get a pension, and a DB pension at that, as are their counterparts in the private sector, and the typical pension is far more generous. And the pension gap will continue to widen, because governments pump far more money into employee pensions than do companies. Civil servants earn an average of $12.38 an hour in benefits, about $5 an hour more than private-sector workers, according to the Bureau of Labor Statistics.[5] The difference was just $2.70 an hour in 1995.

State and local governments have enhanced retirement benefits during the past decade, at a time when corporations have cut them because of their cost. Only 18 percent of private workers now have traditional defined benefit pension plans, compared with more than 80 percent of government employees. Contrary to a widely held notion, the extra government benefits aren't compensation for lower pay. Most government workers are paid more than private employees in similar jobs, and the wage gap is growing. Government pensions also permit early retirement at age 50 or 55 with less of a benefit reduction than that imposed by private pensions, and they more often provide automatic cost-of-living increases to benefits.

American governments' generosity could have serious consequences for taxpayers and pensioners. The U.S. government has a bigger unfunded liability for military and civil servant retirement benefits ($4.7 trillion) than it does for Social Security ($4.6 trillion).[6]

The swing from DB to DC pensions has been even more rapid and widespread in the United States than in Canada. Only *26 percent* of paid employees (government and private) were covered by DB plans in 2004, compared to 68 percent in 1992. That ratio has no doubt fallen further, as union membership has declined since 2004 and troubled businesses with huge pension legacies are cutting health-care and other benefits and freezing DB pensions in favour of DC. In Canada, where a larger percentage of the workforce is in the public sector, the 33 percent of workers covered by DB plans represents a relatively moderate drop from the 37 percent a decade ago.

A growing number of corporate leaders, especially in the United States, are assessing the cost of DB retirement plans and coming to more or less the same conclusion: The cost of maintaining these plans is simply too great. Companies freeze plans generally either by locking out new employees—a "soft" freeze, in the lingo of the pension industry—or by halting new enrolments and stopping the accrual of benefits to existing employees—a "hard" freeze. Freezing a pension plan provides clear economic benefits to companies: A hard freeze can cut the annual retirement payout to a worker by more than half.

Payments to most pensioners in a DB plan are calculated using what is referred to as a "final-average defined-benefit formula." The company multiplies the number of years worked by the average of the worker's three highest years of pay times an accrual rate of 1 to 2 percent, depending, among other things, on the employee contribution. For example, Canadian federal public service workers have an accrual rate of 2 percent, while the U.S. federal employees' rate is 1.1 percent. But the contribution rate is higher for Canadian workers (4 percent versus 0.8 percent for U.S. federal employees). According to the benefits firm Watson Wyatt, the average accrual rate in the United States in 2003 was 1.6 percent. Also, most DB pensions adjust their payments for the cost of living on an annual basis.[7]

Let's do some arithmetic. For an employee retiring after 35 years of service with an average three-year pre-tax income high of $100,000 and an accrual rate of 1.6 percent, the annual pre-tax pension would be valued at: $100,000 \times 35 \times 0.016 = \$56,000$, which amounts to 56 percent of working annual income (this assumes there is no continuing provision for a surviving spouse and no offset for government pension income). Add another five years of work and the benefit would rise to 64 percent of pre-retirement income. If this employee, working for 35 years, retires at age 65 and lives to 85, the total benefit paid would be $1.12 million before any cost-of-living adjustments. If he or she works for 40 years, retires at age 65 and lives to 85, the total benefit paid would be $1.28 million before any cost-of-living adjustments.

DB Plans Are Worth So Much More than DC Plans

DB plans are hugely valuable to the employee. Consider the following example that compares the two types of pension plans:

Two individuals are planning for retirement. Both begin their careers at age 25 and plan to retire at 65, having completed 40 years on the job. Each begins at a starting annual salary of $40,000 and their salaries increase at a rate of 2.5 percent per year. Their average annual income over their last five working years is therefore $102,290.

Now consider two different standard pension plan options, both based on the scenario given above:

Dick is employed by a bank and is covered by a traditional DB plan into which he contributes 2 percent of his salary each year. At age 65, his annual retirement benefit is calculated according to the following formula: Annual Benefit = (Average Income of Last 5 Years) × (Number of Years Worked) × (1.25 percent or 0.0125). We see that the bank uses an accrual rate of 1.25 percent. (For simplicity, we will ignore the annual cost-of-living adjustment, which is commonly given in such plans.)

Jane works for an investment bank and is covered by a DC plan. While contributions to this plan are voluntary, and many low-income or young workers don't make contributions, Jane contributes 2 percent of her income, just like Dick, into a registered (tax-deferred) account to get the 2 percent matching contribution made by her employer.

When Dick turns 65, he is entitled to receive an annual retirement benefit of $51,145. It will be paid until he dies, and then 60 percent of it will be paid to Dick's wife (if she outlives him) until her death. This is an annuity; it continues for the rest of their lives. According to most financial planners, the value of this income stream at age 65 is about 20 times the annual payment, or $1,022,900. In other words, it would take a $1.02 million portfolio to generate with high probability an annual income of $51,145 for an indefinite period into the future, which could be

30 years or even more. This calculation is consistent with a total annual rate of return of 5 percent.

For Jane's registered retirement account to reach the same imputed value of $1.02 million, Jane would have to get an average annual rate of return during her working years of roughly 10.1 percent. This is not likely. Instead, assuming a more realistic 5 percent rate of return, Jane would have to contribute 11.8 percent of her income every year, with the first 2 percent matched by the company, to bring her DC plan up to the $1.02 million mark at retirement.

So Jane has two ways to achieve the same level of financial health in retirement as that enjoyed by Dick. She needs an average annual return of 10.1 percent over her working life (not likely), or, assuming a more realistic 5 percent rate of return, she has to save an additional *9.8 percent* of her income on top of the 2 percent contribution she already makes to get her company matching. This, too, is very difficult; saving 11.8 percent of gross income is quite a hefty chunk. Whichever way you look at it, the DB plan is very valuable, far more so than the DC plan. Dick's plan costs him 2 percent of his income each year, and for the equivalent value Jane's plan costs her 11.8 percent. In order to equalize their compensation, Jane's nominal pre-tax income needs to be 9.8 percent higher than Dick's, year in and year out. That would give her an average annual income of $112,314 in her last five years of work, compared to Dick's $102,290.

Let's look at the example another way. In order to generate a nominal pre-tax income in retirement of $51,145 per year for 20 years—dying at age 85—you would need a nest egg of about $637,000 the day you stop working, assuming a nominal return of 5 percent per year and no bequest. This is the present value of a $51,145 annuity, paid annually at 5 percent for 20 years.

But the fact is that neither you nor your employer knows how many years you will live beyond retirement. So, to be prudent, you must have an even larger nest egg to replace the DB pension, and most financial planners recommend a value of at least 20 times your desired annual income, or $1.02 million in this case, to be certain you do not run out of money before you die based on historical patterns of rates of return.

Of course, if you don't run into a sustained bear market, then, as you get older, you can begin to spend more. But to be sure you don't outlive your money, financial planners now recommend a withdrawal rate of no more than 4 to 5 percent.[8] Amassing even $637,000 of investible savings over a career with peak income of just over $112,000 is not easy, particularly if you've had a couple of kids and bought a house along the way. It would require average annual savings of 8.6 percent of income, or about $5,880 on average (assuming an average annual return of 5 percent and the same income assumptions outlined above). To amass the $1.02 million, you would have to save 13.8 percent of annual income, or $9,436 annually, on average. So the savings rate ranges between 8.6 percent and 13.8 percent.

This can be achieved in a non-taxable account as long as your 2007 income isn't higher than about $105,555 given that the contribution limit on RRSPs is 18 percent of income to a maximum of $19,000 including any company matching contribution. We see that 18 percent of $105,555.55 hits the maximum of $19,000. In future years, the limit will rise $1,000 per year. Currently, the Federal Income Tax Act administered by the Canada Revenue Agency (CRA) has set the total RRSP contribution limit until 2010, when it will hit $22,000. After that, it is intended to rise by the cost of living, although this schedule is of course subject to change, as the federal government can choose to alter limits (likely raising them) in the future.[9]

For a 401(k), the American version of the RRSP, the maximum employee contribution set by the Internal Revenue Service (IRS) is $15,500 for the year 2007. For future years the limit will be indexed for inflation, increasing in increments of $500.[10] Plans set up under section 401(k) can also have employer contributions that, when added to the employee contributions, cannot exceed the lesser of 100 percent of the employee's compensation or $45,000 for 2007.[11] The employer matching contribution in the United States is typically about 50 cents on the dollar up to 6 percent of your salary. It would therefore take a $1 million income to hit the $45,000 total limit—the employee maximum contribution of $15,500 and the remaining $30,000 is the 50 cents match on the dollar up to 6 percent of $1 million. Now, consider what would happen if the bank had frozen the DB pension plan when Dick was 50, having been on the job for 25 years. Dick's average salary for the five years before the freeze was $70,600. Upon retirement at age 65, his benefit would be just $22,063 a year (70,600 × 25 × 1.25 percent), a shortfall of $29,083 a year from what he would have received had the plan not been frozen. At 85, the total benefit paid out before the cost-of-living adjustment would be $441,260, or $581,640 less than the total benefit had the pension not been frozen. However, companies rarely freeze their pension plans outright without introducing some form of offsetting 401(k) contribution plan. IBM, for example (having frozen its DB plan), now matches 401(k) contributions dollar-for-dollar up to 6 percent of the employee's income, which will still save the company an estimated $3 billion by the end of 2010.[12]

For all those workers whose DB pensions have been hard frozen, a significant rise in personal savings would be needed to make up the difference. If we assume that the $29,083 difference in annual retirement income is worth $581,660 at age 65 (the 20-times-the-annual-payment rule again), then the 50-year-old worker whose pension was frozen in the above example would have to save almost $27,000 annually in an RRSP or 401(k), at 5 percent for 15 years, to make up the gap. This works out to about 29 percent of his average income over this period. Of course, this amount would be reduced if the company began a DC-plan matching program, but the burden would still be substantial.

Even companies whose traditional pensions are fully funded—meaning they have enough assets on hand to cover the benefits of all participants—are freezing plans in the United States. They are doing so because retirees are living longer, raising overall costs, and because U.S. pension-accounting rules require companies to deduct their plans' shortfalls from net worth. Subsidiaries of U.S.-based firms, companies that are listed on U.S. stock exchanges, and companies that have issued debt in the United States are required to comply with the new Generally Accepted Accounting Principles (GAAP) rules. The majority of Canadian private sector pension plan sponsors will have to comply. The Certified General Accountants Association of Canada reported in late 2005 that the estimated shortfall in the nation's DB plans increased from $160 billion at the end of 2003 to $190 billion at the end of 2004.[13]

More recently, after years of underfunding, the health of pension plans has improved considerably, thanks to strong stock market returns, five-fold increases in company contributions since 1999, and rising interest rates. The pension plans of Fortune 100 companies ended 2006 with 102.4 percent of the

assets needed to pay pensions indefinitely, according to one estimate reported in *The Wall Street Journal*.[14] That is up sharply
from a low point of 81.9 percent in 2002, though still below the
125.8 percent recorded at the height of the stock-market boom in
1999. A similar improvement has occurred in pension funding
in Canada.

Fewer pension plans are at risk of failing, which is very good
news for retirees. One question remains, however: How big a role
have pension freezes and cuts played in improving pension
funding? Freezing or cutting benefits reduces a company's
pension liabilities, which means the existing assets cover more of
the company's obligations.

From 2003 to 2006, 71 Fortune 1000 pension plans have been
terminated or frozen in the United States, a sharp increase from

Chart 25

Number of Plan Freezes and Terminations
Freezes/Terminations of Defined Benefit Plans—
Fortune 1000 Companies

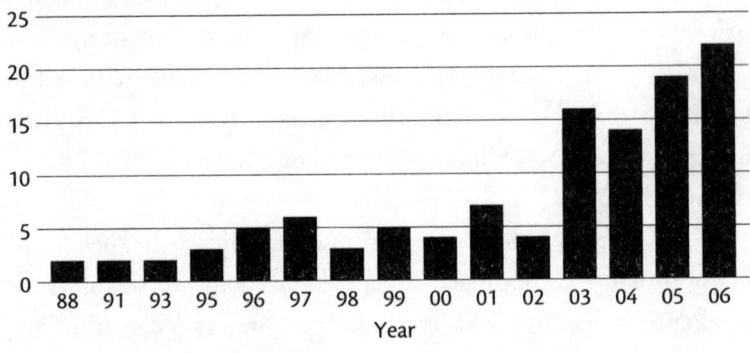

Year

the rate we've seen since the late 1980s (Chart 25).[15] Many of these have come from healthy businesses, including Verizon, Motorola, Hewlett-Packard, IBM, Alcoa, and DuPont.

Americans Worry More, but Affluent Canadians Should as Well

These trends might help explain why Americans appear more anxious about retirement than Canadians do. Numerous studies in the United States suggest that many boomers are financially unprepared. Almost half of American working-age households— given current savings rates and changes in pensions and Social Security—are at risk of being unable to maintain their standard of living in retirement. A June 2006 study by the Center for Retirement Research at Boston College provides some of the clearest evidence to date that many Americans are doing far too little to prepare financially for their golden years and are unaware of how their lives might change.[16] The situation is not hopeless, but it requires many people, especially the higher-income earners, to save more money and push back their planned retirement dates. If anything, the study might understate the problem. It assumes people will retire at 65, when many Americans actually retire earlier; it also assumes that families will annuitize their wealth, including taking a reverse mortgage on their homes for additional financial support.

People are living longer, traditional pensions are disappearing, savings rates are anaemic in both personal accounts and 401(k)s, and the point at which people qualify for full Social Security benefits is rising gradually to age 67 for those born in 1960 or later. Yet many Americans under 60 do not understand the full implications of these developments for their own retirement; after all, their parents and grandparents retired quite comfortably. Many are deluding themselves into a false sense of security. According to a study recently conducted for a large U.S. insurer, 40 percent of those surveyed weren't sure how much they could safely withdraw from a retirement portfolio, and an additional 29 percent thought that a safe retirement withdrawal rate was 10 percent or more.[17] Financial planners today believe the number is no more than 5 percent. As an over-indebted generation comes closer and closer to the end of their full-time careers, there is a large gap between expectation and reality.

For Canada, a Statscan study using 1999 data from the Survey of Financial Security finds that a third of families age 45 to 64 may not have saved enough for their retirement.[18] This study assumes that two-thirds of pre-retirement income is sufficient to maintain living standards. If, instead, 80 percent of pre-retirement earnings should be replaced to meet retirement goals, an estimated 44 percent of family units have a savings deficiency. The higher your employment income, the more you will have to rely on private sources to maintain your lifestyle in retirement. Low-income households, for example, will likely find CPP, Old Age Security, and the Guaranteed Income Supplement sufficient.

Roughly 41 percent of Canadian households earning $75,000 a year or more might not be able to replace two-thirds of their earnings; and a whopping 55 percent of Canadian high-income households have not saved enough to replace 80 percent of their employment income. The problem is less acute for the self-employed if they are able to realize the equity in their business as a source of retirement income. Owning your own home mortgage-free makes a big difference, as it is assumed that one-half of the equity is an asset from which retirement income can be generated. With this assumption, only 15 percent of Canadian debt-free homeowners appear to have saved too little to replace two-thirds of their employment income. In comparison, 34 percent of homeowners with a mortgage may come up short.

Many profligate boomers are asking themselves if they will ever be in a position to stop working, particularly those who are not covered by a DB pension plan. While relatively more of the oldest boomers are covered by such plans, the bulk of all boomers are not. What's more, the person who spends 30 years or more with a single employer is increasingly the exception, not the rule. In today's competitive global marketplace, many manufacturing and even service-sector jobs in Canada and the United States have been outsourced to low-wage countries, and restructuring and layoffs have been much more prevalent than they were for boomer parents.

Government pensions—CPP or Social Security—were never intended to replace most of employment income. The CPP is intended to cover about 25 percent of the income on which premiums were paid. The median level of total Canadian family income is $58,100 per household. For higher-income earners, CPP will be woefully inadequate to maintain working living standards. So the richer you are, the more you will need to rely on private pensions, either DB or DC registered employment pensions or your own savings in registered or non-registered accounts.

Social Security is about twice as generous as CPP, but U.S. seniors are burdened with far higher medical payments than Canadians are, and they pay more in employee contributions. American seniors pay for medical costs that are not covered by Medicare, and these costs are rising sharply. Health insurance for seniors is very expensive, and increasing numbers of U.S. employers are limiting their health benefits for pensioners. Some businesses are allocating a set dollar figure, which, depending on health and longevity, might be sufficient or might fall very far short; other companies have radically reduced their health benefits for employees and pensioners. This is becoming common in the airline and automobile industries, which have, in some cases, taken on the unions to reduce labour costs. Since 2004 there has been a marked slowdown in the rise in employer benefits costs, as U.S. employees are now digging into their own pockets to pick up the tab for a larger share of health care.

With the rising importation of products from low-wage countries, especially China, domestic businesses in Canada and the United States have restructured extensively to increase productivity growth and profit margins in an extraordinarily competitive business environment (Chart 26). Few have the ability to pass along rising costs to the consumer, and many are suffering from

Chart 26

Productivity and Profit Margins

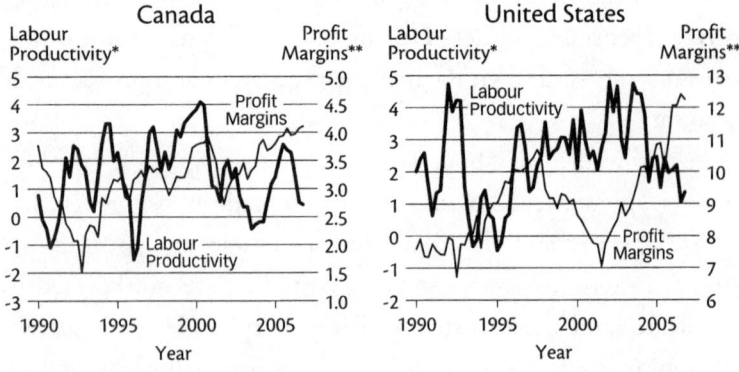

* Business Sector (y/y % change)   ** Operating Profits / GDP (percent)

Sources: Statistics Canada, BEA.

the rise in energy prices. When searching for ways to reduce costs, the primary targets have been wages, salaries, and benefits, and that, of course, includes pensions.

Pension Comparisons by Country

The Organisation for Economic Co-operation and Development (OECD) calculates, by country, the degree to which pensions cover pre-retirement after-tax income in an attempt to analyze the potential financial health of the growing number of retirees in the developed world (Table 4). The analysis covers all mandatory pension schemes—not only public pension systems, but also all compulsory private pensions. It also examines safety nets for the elderly and takes account of differences in taxes between countries. The analysis compares the net replacement rate of three

Table 4

Income Replacement Rates in the OECD
2005

Country	Net Repl. Rate by Income			Country	Net Repl. Rate by Income		
	Low (0.5×)	Mid (1.0×)	High (2.0×)		Low (0.5×)	Mid (1.0×)	High (2.0×)
Australia	77.0	52.4	36.5	Japan	80.1	59.1	44.3
Austria	91.2	93.2	79.3	Luxembourg	125.0	109.8	104.2
Canada	89.4	57.1	30.6	Mexico	50.4	45.1	44.1
Finland	87.3	71.5	123.1	Netherlands	82.5	84.1	83.8
France	98.0	68.8	59.2	New Zealand	77.1	39.5	22.0
Germany	61.7	71.8	67.0	Norway	85.5	65.1	50.1
Greece	99.9	99.9	99.9	Slovak Rep.	58.2	60.2	65.7
Hungary	86.6	90.5	92.6	United Kingdom	78.4	47.6	29.8
Ireland	63.0	36.6	21.9	United States	61.4	51.0	39.0
Italy	89.3	88.8	89.1				

Individual pension entitlement as a percent of
pre-retirement earnings, net of taxes and contributions.

Source: OECD.

different income categories: "low," which is defined as half of average income; "average"; and "high," which is double the average income.

For average income earners, Canada and the United States have low replacement rates relative to most other OECD countries, at 57.1 percent and 51.0 percent, respectively. In Canada, the equivalent of 89.4 percent of pre-retirement income is replaced for low-income earners. In France, the replacement rate is a whopping 98 percent for this income category, and in Luxembourg it is 125 percent, which I suppose means that older poor people in Luxembourg are better looked after than younger poor people. For the United States, the low-income replacement rate is the third lowest in the OECD at 61.4 percent—ahead of only the Slovak Republic and Mexico—quite a sad state of affairs, especially given the widening income gap between rich and poor.

For average-income earners, Canada's replacement rate is well below Austria's, for example, which is at 93.2 percent, and Greece's, at 100 percent. Average-income earners in the United States again receive a relatively low rate; only in Ireland, Mexico, New Zealand, and the United Kingdom are the rates lower.

At the high end of the income spectrum, the replacement rate in Canada falls to just 30.6 percent, quite low compared to most other developed countries, and below the U.S. level of 39 percent. From these data we confirm that *the higher-income folks are the ones who must rely most heavily on non-mandatory sources of wealth accumulation to fund most of their retirement income,* by making maximum contributions to RRSPs and 401(k)s as well as non-registered savings. We also see that Canada is better at protecting the poor than the United States at the expense of the rich, which makes sense; Canada's system creates a flatter income distribution than in the United States, where the gap between rich and poor is wider and widening. But as generous as Canada is in comparison to our neighbours to the south, our coverage is nowhere near that of the welfare states of Austria, Finland, Greece, Hungary, Italy, the Netherlands, and Turkey.

Caution in Caring
for Retirement Savings

Ironically, at a time when global economic well-being has never been greater, risk today might be higher than reflected by the financial markets, given geopolitical clashes, proliferation of nuclear capability, terrorism, extreme weather conditions, and a host of other factors. The developing world is growing rapidly, particularly in Asia. Interest rates, though up from their lows of 2005, are still low by the historical standards of much of the seventies and eighties; inflation has trended downward since the mid-eighties, albeit with some interim volatility; and there is far too little extra financial return paid to investors willing to take more risk. For example, the rate of return on high-yield bonds that are less than investment grade—so-called "junk" bonds—is not sufficiently above the yield on the safest government bonds (of equal maturity) to warrant exposing your savings to the additional risk in the junk bond market.

Stock, bond, and currency markets seem to account only partially for the greater risk associated with owning lower-grade financial assets; the spread between the returns on these invest-ments relative to blue chip, large-cap stocks and the bonds issued by very-high-quality corporations or triple-A governments (those with the highest credit rating or, equivalently, the least likelihood of defaulting) is very low. This is because there is so much money in the world chasing higher yields.

As a result, it pays to be cautious, and pre-retirees are wise to make more conservative assumptions than in earlier decades about likely future rates of return. Younger people, as well, must plan for increased risk in their careers, businesses, and investments, as firms adjust quickly to shifting economic pressures. Keep in mind that the funds in DC accounts (RRSPs) are precious dollars. They grow at tax-free rates, but if you suffer a capital loss, it can't be used to offset a capital gain. And when you withdraw the money in retirement, you must pay ordinary income tax on all of it, even if some was the result of dividends and capital gains. Money in your RRSP grows tax-free until you begin to withdraw it in retirement. So you don't want to take unnecessary risk in your RRSP. While you must pay tax in the year when dividends are received or capital gains are realized for non-registered accounts, at least dividends and capital gains are taxed at preferential (lower) rates, and capital losses can be used to offset capital gains in the future. This is called a capital loss carry-forward, which offsets future years' capital gains until the full amount of the loss is used up.

Since 1998, when tech stocks took off and then imploded, technological growth and innovations have hardly stood still: Y2K mania came and went; "Google" and "TiVo" became verbs; cable systems rolled out 800 channels; satellite transformed radio; cameras went digital; flat screen high-density TVs entered the mainstream; Apple kneecapped the CD and cellphone industries; Starbucks installed Wi-Fi; and computers got much faster and better. Yet, in the aggregate, less money was made on the Nasdaq on balance—the index most associated with large-cap tech stocks— than on the S&P 500 or the Dow Jones Industrial Average.

On the other hand, the Toronto Stock Exchange (TSX) index has more than doubled over this period, reflecting Canada's surge in energy and materials stocks and the strong performance in the financial services sector. In addition, the Canadian dollar has appreciated against the U.S. dollar since early 2002, rising more than 50 percent by mid-2007. In consequence, the total exchange-rate-adjusted return on the S&P 500 for Canadian investors was *minus* 19 percent since the end of 1998, compared to the 118 percent gain right here at home.

The Future Looks Good for High-Quality Dividend-Paying Stocks

As the oldest boomers push through their 60s, an army of financial planners and investment consultants is mobilized to guide their clients out of equities and into bonds in an effort to offer them income and stability. History has been their guide. Income-oriented investors have enjoyed a secular bull market in bonds over the past 25 years. Over that period, the 10-year Government of Canada (GoC) bond rate dropped from 14 percent to just over 4 percent. Inflation in 1981 was 12.4 percent. Now it is generally meeting the Bank of Canada target of 2 percent for core inflation. Clearly, the past 25 years have been favourable for bond investors. A portfolio of long-term government and corporate bonds returned to the investor a compounded annualized return of about 12.5 percent, compared to 9.5 percent for the TSX over that period.

There is zero likelihood that the next 25 years will offer the same return for bond investors. Now that interest rates and inflation are so historically low, traditional bond portfolios will have a difficult time providing an acceptable level of income while protecting purchasing power over the next 25 to 30 years.

The Bank of Canada and the Federal Reserve have driven down inflation over this period. But while Canada is in the

enviable and unique position among the G8 countries of having
a surplus in both trade and budget balances, the United States
suffers from enormous international imbalances (Chart 27). The
current account deficit in the United States has finally resulted in
a multi-year fall in the U.S. dollar. This has led to a rise in the cost
of imports and an inherent inflation bias. Protectionism, always
popular during an election period, could also trigger inflation
pressure.

Moreover, with a nearly $250 billion federal budget deficit in
2006, interest rates would rise sharply in the United States if it
weren't for the enormous inflow of foreign capital to the U.S.
bond market.[19] More than half of all U.S. Treasury bills and
bonds outstanding are owned by foreigners, compared to only
13 percent for GoCs (Chart 28). We have already seen a sharp
decline in Japanese buying of Treasuries; much of the money

Chart 27

Current Account Balances ... Separate Ways
Current Account Balances (% of nominal GDP)

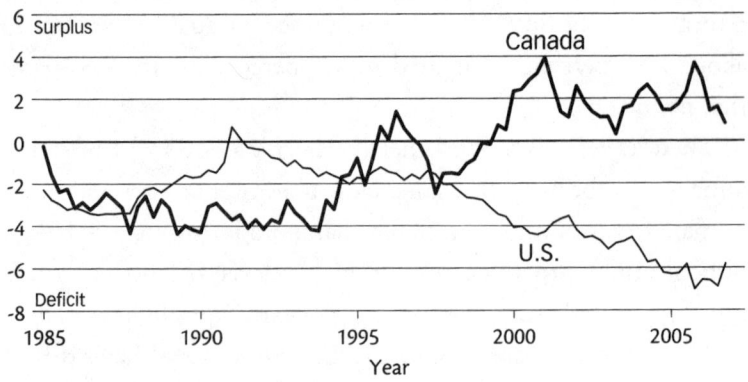

Sources: Statistics Canada, BEA.

coming from Britain originates in the oil-rich countries of the Middle East; and China is now the largest net purchaser of Treasuries. This is clearly a reflection of China's effort to peg the yuan at an undervalued level. The purchase of Treasuries with yuan increases the demand for U.S. dollars relative to the demand for the Chinese currency, thereby maintaining the peg. This is an unstable situation and many countries have already begun to diversify their reserve holdings away from U.S. Treasury securities, helping to put some modest upward pressure on interest rates.

The United States has been pressuring China to revalue its currency for some time in an effort to reduce the bilateral trade deficit. But we should be careful what we wish for. If the Chinese were to allow their currency to rise sharply, their net exports to the United States might well decline, but so would their net purchases of Treasury securities. If the slide was dramatic, bond

Chart 28

U.S. Most Reliant on Foreign Capital
Foreign Ownership of Government Bonds
(% of total privately-held)

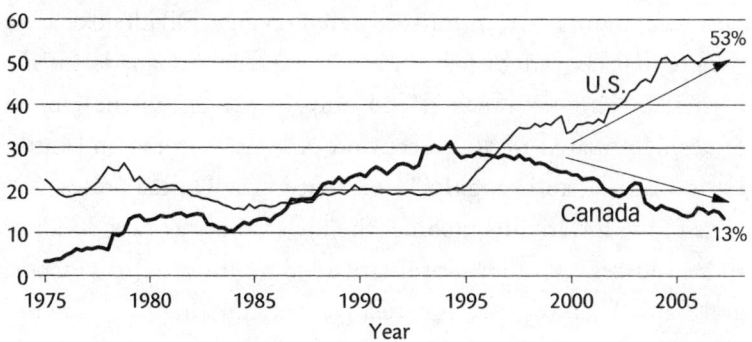

Sources: Statistics Canada, BEA.

yields could rise sharply unless the Congress and the White House slashed the budget deficit. This is hardly likely during the "war on terror," and either fiscal or monetary tightening would ultimately slow the economy.

Retirees, therefore, need to rethink the traditional bond portfolio as a holistic income solution. Given the economic backdrop, investors should be looking at a more diversified approach to income generation and inflation protection. Recent analysis now suggests that a portfolio of about 50 percent stocks (mostly large-cap equities) and 50 percent bonds (mostly government or high-quality corporate bonds) has the best chance of achieving *portfolio longevity*, defined as the number of years a portfolio can sustain withdrawals of about 4 to 5 percent in real terms before all its assets are exhausted. Most financial planners suggest that a 65-year-old retiree should be looking for portfolio longevity of 30 years.[20] I will discuss this in greater detail in the next chapter.

Dividends Matter

Stocks should be included in all investment accounts, especially high-quality dividend-paying stocks. This is particularly true in taxable accounts—your non-registered savings. Dividends have a preferential tax rate of just under 25 percent in Canada for the highest income-tax bracket (and only 15 percent in the United States), compared to 46 percent on ordinary income and interest in Canada, and roughly 35 percent in the United States. (Of course, the lower your income, the lower your tax rate on all of these sources of funds—ordinary income, interest, dividends, and capital gains—but the relative tax rates remain similar.) Canadian capital gains tax rates are roughly 23 percent (and only

15 percent in the United States, if gains are from securities held for over a year).

Remember, however, that investments accumulating tax-free in a registered retirement account (RRSPs and 401(k)s) are subject to ordinary income tax rates when the money is withdrawn. For many, income from this source will be lower in retirement, which might reduce your marginal tax rate. In addition, any capital losses in an RRSP or 401(k) are not permitted to offset capital gains in other investment portfolios.

Many people save for retirement beyond their registered accounts, taking advantage of the preferential tax treatment of dividends and capital gains, as well as the offset of capital losses. The trade-off depends on how long the RRSP or 401(k) will go untouched—the longer it does, the greater the value of the tax-free accumulation of interest and dividends—and the value of the immediate income-tax deductibility of the contribution. Most affluent boomers without a DB pension plan will find that even maximum contributions to an RRSP or 401(k) over their 30-year career will not be enough of a nest egg to assure prudent portfolio longevity, especially given the low contribution limits on these accounts in their early years. Their retirement savings will likely consist of both taxable and non-taxable accounts.

An Example of a Dividend Stock Screen

Blue-chip dividend-paying stocks should be considered in a long-term investment portfolio, including during retirement. The most favourable are those stocks with an attractive yield, a history of steady dividend growth above the rate of inflation, a low payout ratio, and an improving position in the marketplace. These stocks are particularly attractive to individuals in or near retirement, when real income growth is a priority and the favourable tax treatment of dividends is of considerable importance in taxable accounts. Such stocks are arguably safer than corporate bonds and have the advantage of both growth and income. Private equity funds have bought companies and issued corporate bonds to pay back the equity position. For example, HCA (Hospital Corporation of America) bonds fell 14 percent after the announcement of its buyout in July 2006. Furthermore, steady dividend payers perform relatively well during periods of slowing economic growth, as their stable earnings and dividend stream attract a premium multiple.

Table 5 shows the results of a dividend stock screening of Canadian and U.S. publicly listed companies using the following criteria:

1. must be a member of TSX or S&P 500 index
2. dividend yield must be greater than 2.5 percent
3. five-year dividend growth must be greater than 10 percent
4. payout ratio must be less than 60 percent
5. must have a positive 10-year trend in pre-tax profit margin
6. beta must be less than 1 (Beta is a measure of the volatility, or systematic risk, of a security in comparison to the market as a whole. A low beta means low systemic risk.)

This example is meant to be illustrative only; it is not a stock recommendation. It is shown to give you a sense of the alternative high-quality dividend payers out there. Other considerations include sector risk, exchange-rate risk, your own risk profile, and other personal and financial factors. Your investment adviser or financial planner can devise a screen to meet your personal requirements and preferences.

Table 5

Dividend Stock Screen

(ranked in order of market cap : as of July 9, 2007)

	Symb.	Company	Market Cap. ($blns)	Sector	Div. Yield (%)	5-Yr Div. Growth (%)	Payout Ratio	Beta
TSX	RY	Royal Bank of Canada	C$77	Financial	3.0	15.6	44.5	0.58
	BNS	Bank of Nova Scotia	54	Financial	3.1	19.7	41.4	0.61
	BMO	Bank of Montreal	35	Financial	3.9	14.3	39.0	0.52
	GWO	Great-West Life	32	Financial	2.8	19.6	41.5	0.65
	PWF	Power Financial	30	Financial	2.7	18.4	38.2	0.76
	IGM	IGM Financial	15	Financial	3.0	16.4	51.8	0.90
	NA	National Bank	10	Financial	3.3	18.9	34.5	0.61
	RET/A	Reitmans	2	Consumer Disc.	2.6	39.1	34.6	0.75
S&P 500	BAC	Bank of America	US$228	Financial	4.4	13.2	45.7	0.63
	JNJ	Johnson & Johnson	184	Health Care	2.7	15.8	38.6	0.34
	WFC	Wells Fargo	122	Financial	3.1	16.7	42.9	0.38
	KO	Coca-Cola	122	Consumer Stpl	2.6	11.5	57.3	0.60
	WB	Wachovia Corporation	108	Financial	4.0	17.4	46.3	0.72
	KMB	Kimberly-Clark	33	Consumer Stpl	3.0	11.8	60.0	0.46
	BBT	BB&T Corporation	24	Financial	3.9	10.3	57.8	0.48
	WMI	Waste Management	20	Industrial	2.5	131.2	30.9	0.88
	PPL	PPL Corporation	18	Utilities	2.7	15.7	47.6	0.42
	CINF	Cincinnati Financial	8	Financial	3.0	12.0	24.9	0.71

Criteria: member of TSX or S&P 500; dividend yield > 2.5%;
5-year dividend growth > 10%; payout ratio < 60%;
Beta < 1 (for a risk measure); positive 10-year trend in pre-tax margin

Source: Bloomberg data.

A Fool's Game: Timing Markets

An analysis by Burton Malkiel, author of the classic book *A Random Walk Down Wall Street,* shows that from 1970 to 1994, mutual-fund managers—professionals in the business—were incorrect in their allocation of assets into cash in essentially every market cycle.[21] In other words, they became more cautious at troughs in the stock market and shifted more money into cash. Conversely, they became less cautious, reducing cash allocations, almost invariably at market peaks. If *they* can't time markets, you have to ask yourself, how can you?

Markets, by definition, respond the most to unexpected events or developments; if these events are expected, they are already "in the market," reflected in current price levels. Moreover, markets are a discounting mechanism. They anticipate the future, and today's valuations encompass (discount) what the market expects is yet to come. Occasionally, you or your adviser might be better than the market at predicting the future; then you stand a chance of outperforming the stock index over the period about which you have been prescient. But this is very risky business; mistakes are costly, and trading generates significant transactions costs (not to mention tax liabilities in a taxable account), which could well wipe out your gain. Generally, performance data suggest that about 80 percent of timers fail over any reasonable period of time.[22]

Chart 29

Miss the Best 10 Days Each Year . . .

TSX (as of September 25, 2007)

. . . Wipe Out All of Your Return

Source: BMO Capital Markets

Gains in the stock market can be quick and sharp. If you miss the best 10 days in the market each year, you wipe out all of the return and actually lose money. For example, since 1996, the TSX has risen nearly 200 percent. If you exclude the top 10 days each year, however, the index would be down 70 percent (Chart 29). See how crucial those up days are? And no one sends you an email the night before, telling you it's time to buy.

Looking at this another way, since 1970 nearly 100 percent of the capital gains in the S&P 500 were made in only 10 percent of the months; during the remaining 90 percent of the months, the index fell sharply in just under half of them and posted ho-hum returns in the rest.

It is even tougher to time the highly cyclical TSX, as substantial gains were made in only about 8 percent of the months since the mid-seventies; the stock index plunged 20 percent or more in over 25 percent of the months, declined less sharply in 17 percent of the months, and posted modest changes the remaining 50 percent of the time. What are the chances of catching those rare months when returns surge if you are in and out of the market? Miss those great months, or even days, and you can turn a winning portfolio into a losing one.

So ensure that your portfolio is well diversified and invest regularly during your wealth-accumulation years to take advantage of dollar-cost averaging. Attempting to time markets is a fool's game, particularly when investing for the long term. Some people feel they can increase the return on their portfolio through *active equity investment.* Passive investing seeks to replicate the performance of a group of financial assets. Examples of this approach are index mutual funds or (less costly) ETFs (exchange-traded funds) or even a diversified, conservative, buy-and-hold strategy. Active investing seeks to earn above-average returns, usually by selecting individual securities that are expected to outperform the benchmarks and trading them more aggressively.

It is possible to enjoy outsized returns with this method, particularly if you have access to excellent investment advice and the time to study it and follow the markets closely. However, active investment, while maybe rewarding, is also risky. You can expect more volatility, and you must be prepared to see inevitable losses as well as gains. Most long-term investors prefer more stable returns, but some relatively small portion of your portfolio could well be managed actively if you have the time, knowledge, and courage to handle the risk.

KEY POINTS

- Increasingly fewer workers are covered by traditional defined benefit (DB) pension plans, as the cost to employers has risen sharply with the rise in life expectancy.

- Even if you have a DB plan, often the benefits are capped at a particular income level. For those who earn substantially more than the income cap, the plan alone will not be sufficient to maintain living standards in retirement. Further savings will be required to finance the additional income needed.

- These days, defined contribution (DC) plans (such as RRSPs) are more the norm, which shifts the risk and the cost of providing an income flow during retirement to the employee.

- Canada's retirement system is effectively two-tiered, with public sector workers guaranteed fully indexed pensions, while private sector workers will be lucky to have a pension at all.

- It is a similar story in the United States, where the pension gap will continue to widen as governments pump more money into gold-plated pension plans than companies can afford. The DB pension plan is nearly extinct in the private sector in the United States, and an estimated half to two-thirds of Canadian businesses with DB plans are thinking about less-costly provisions or alternatives.

- Most recent data indicate that many boomers have not saved enough for retirement, particularly the more affluent ones who carry too much debt, live high on the hog, and want to maintain a relatively high living standard.

- Higher-income earners must rely not just on pension funds but also on taxable savings to fund their retirement needs. Investments should be reasonably cautious, depending on age, and well diversified.

- There are many unsavoury characters who prey on older people, sometimes wiping out their savings. If it seems too good to be true, it probably is. Don't make financial decisions without expert advice from accredited financial planners, investment advisers, lawyers, or accountants, depending on the issue. A disinterested expert who makes no money directly from your decisions should be consulted for your overall financial plan.

- For boomers with family income of twice the median level, mandatory government pensions and the social safety net will cover only about 31 percent of their income in retirement. The higher your income, the lower the coverage ratio.

- For those with household income at the median level, today at just over $58,000, 57 percent is covered. For poor families, 89 percent or more is covered.

- This is a very fair, progressive system, but it means that relatively affluent families must save significant amounts for their retirement security. Even with many DB pension plans, income caps are set, so it is the individual's responsibility to make up the difference.

- High-quality dividend-paying stocks will be an attractive investment for many boomers, especially in non-registered accounts where you can take advantage of the preferential tax treatment of dividends and capital gains compared to ordinary income and interest.

- Don't try to time markets. Few can do it consistently and successfully, and you could deplete your potential savings by missing the best days in the market. Besides, you would run up significant commission fees. Needless to say, don't day trade or take inordinate risk with your retirement savings.

- Investors should look at a diversified approach to income generation and inflation protection. A portfolio of about 50 percent stocks (especially high-quality dividend-paying stocks) and 50 percent bonds has the best chance of achieving portfolio longevity.

Chapter 9

How Much Is Enough? Nest Egg Arithmetic

Nothing worries pre-retirees more than not having enough money to maintain their living standard in retirement. All of us hope to have a long, happy, healthy, and financially secure retirement, but given the risks we confront—longevity risk, income risk, and contingency risk—most people have no real idea what a prudent size of nest egg is and whether it can be accumulated in time. We have already discussed ways to reduce financial needs during retirement. These would include working at least part-time until later in life, moving to a less expensive home or locale, paying down all of your debt before retirement, dispensing with unnecessary overhead, using a portion of your free time to do some of the things you hire others to do now, and maybe choosing to take the time to hunt for bargains and comparison shop. The internet makes comparison shopping relatively easy. You might find you eat out less because you have more time to cook. You probably don't need as extensive a wardrobe. You will have eliminated commuting and other job-related costs, and you won't be contributing to CPP, Employment Insurance, or retirement savings plans. Most likely, your children will be off the family payroll, although many boomers choose to help their kids buy their first home and save for their grandchildren's education.

All of that might help, but to be prudent you should figure out, as best you can, how much pre-tax annual income you will need during retirement. Subtract from that amount any income you will receive from government and private pensions, and from any other sources (such as rents on real estate). Once you agree (with the help of a financial planner or adviser) on a ballpark estimate, you can use a very reliable rule of thumb to determine the appropriate size of your nest egg to generate that additional desired pre-tax income.

> **RULE OF THUMB:** You will need a retirement nest egg of between 20 and 25 times the level of additional desired pre-tax income (over and above government and employment pensions) to generate the extra income you need.

This is a conservative rule, allowing you to withdraw between 4 and 5 percent of your nest egg in your first year of retirement. Your financial adviser can help you decide where in this range you can prudently begin.

Each subsequent year, you can increase your withdrawal rate by the rate of inflation, say, roughly 3 percent per year. So if your withdrawal rate begins at 4.1 percent in Year 1, it can prudently rise to 4.22 percent (4.1 percent × 1.03) in Year 2, to 4.35 percent in Year 3, to 4.5 percent in Year 4, and so on. In Year 10, in this example, your safe withdrawal rate would be 5.35 percent.

Starting with a 4.1 percent initial withdrawal rate is very conservative. Assuming markets behave in ways similar to what we have experienced since 1926, an initial withdrawal rate of 4.1 percent will assure *with virtual certainty* that you will generate your additional desired pre-tax income for a retirement period of 30 years. This is generally long enough for most people.

We are assuming here a 5 percent average annual rate of return on your portfolio after adjusting for an average inflation rate of 3 percent. History suggests in order to earn this rate of return, you should invest at least half of your nest egg in stocks, with the remainder in bonds. The higher the equity proportion, the higher the safe initial withdrawal rate in the 4 to 5 percent range; but you wouldn't want to choose too many small-cap or speculative stocks. They should make up no more than a third of your equity portfolio. Blue chip large-cap dividend-paying stocks with a good track record of dividend hikes and growth are a very attractive investment vehicle for a portion of the equity component of your retirement savings. Both the stock and bond components should be invested in a diversified portfolio of high-quality assets; you should consider foreign as well as Canadian equity investments, because the Canadian stock market alone might not provide sufficient diversification. Investing in mutual funds or ETFs could diversify your portfolio without requiring specific stock picks. Seek expert advice on these choices.

A number of factors can affect the level of your initial withdrawal rate. If, for example, you are willing to take a bit more longevity risk—assuring your money will last 30 years with, say, a 97 percent probability, you could raise your initial withdrawal rate a bit. We will get into the details below. The shorter your retirement period, the higher your safe initial withdrawal rate. Another factor that affects your safe withdrawal rate (or the size of your nest egg) is whether you are willing to die with very little money left or instead wish to leave a legacy beyond the value of your non-financial assets.

Here Is How It Works

As an example, let's make the following assumptions:

- you retire at age 65 and live to age 90, giving 25 years of retirement,
- your average annual rate of return on your investment portfolio is 8 percent before inflation adjustment,
- inflation is 3 percent over the course of your retirement.

You will need savings equal to only 14 times your desired pre-tax retirement income over and above government or private pensions, if you are willing to die broke (excluding the value of your house).

Under this scenario, you must be willing to dip into your capital little by little over the years, spending your last cent in your ninetieth year. So if, for example, you desired pre-tax retirement income of $50,000 a year over and above your government and other pensions, you would need savings of about $700,000 on your last day of work. Your initial withdrawal rate would be roughly 7 percent, which is equal to 1 divided by 14 (0.0714 to be more exact, or 7.14 percent).

If dying broke bothers you, or you think you might live well beyond age 90, or you want to have a better chance of dying with a legacy of financial assets for your heirs, then the rule of thumb becomes this: *You will need a retirement nest egg of 22 times your desired pre-tax annual income.* In this example, that would be $1.1 million in savings for pre-tax retirement income of $50,000 a year. In either case, dying broke or dying rich, we are assuming you remain roughly 50 percent invested in stocks. Otherwise, you are unlikely to achieve an 8 percent nominal return. The lower the return, and the higher the inflation rate, the more money you will need to meet your income requirements adjusted for inflation, thus the higher the savings multiple.

For another example, if you desire $100,000 in pre-tax retirement income from your investment portfolio, you will need a retirement nest egg of $1.4 million if you are willing to use up all of your capital by age 90, or $2.2 million if you don't want to dip into much of your capital. These calculations can be adjusted for different retirement periods and different nominal and real rate-of-return assumptions. This is exactly what a financial planner does—show you the range of assumptions and their implications.

The bottom line here is that some people might not need to accumulate huge sums of wealth to retire comfortably; but many do. Fortunately, the power of compound returns helps significantly, especially tax-free compounding available in an RRSP or 401(k). Employer-matching contributions help as well. Even the youngest employees should contribute enough to their RRSP to get the maximum amount their employers will contribute. It means that half of your pension balance is free money. Don't pass that up, even if it requires scrimping a bit. Just that small initial contribution in the first few years of employment will compound tax-free to a substantial sum over a 40-year career.

Once your RRSP grows to a value of about twice your income, the tax-free return on your portfolio each year will likely be larger than your annual contribution. In other words, it gets easier to amass large sums of wealth as the years pass. The sooner you start saving, the easier it is. If you can reach an RRSP balance of roughly twice your income by age 40, you are in good shape.

In summary, the steps to financial security in retirement are as follows: calculate or at least guesstimate how much pre-tax income you will need in retirement over and above what you will receive from government or private pensions and any other source (other investments, job or business sources, inheritances, and so on); and determine how much you need to accumulate—using our rule of thumb (described in more detail below)—by the time you retire fully. Then you can work backwards, with the help of an expert, to see what that means in terms of monthly or annual contributions to an RRSP and an investment account.

Rules of thumb, however, necessarily make simplifying assumptions. The reality is that we do not know how long we will be retired, and life expectancy is rising. As well, average rates of return in the future are unpredictable, as markets are volatile. Making conservative assumptions is prudent, because it is not only the average return that is important, but also the *pattern* of returns. If you run into a bear market early in your retirement, you will be forced to sell shares at markedly depressed prices, which would significantly increase your chances of outliving your money. That is why many financial planners recommend including income-generating stocks and bonds in your portfolio and an initial withdrawal rate of only between 4 and 5 percent or, equivalently, a nest egg of 20 to 25 times your desired pre-tax annual income from the portfolio.

If historical experience is any guide, this would virtually eliminate your risk of running out of money over a 30-year retirement period, allowing you to have peace of mind regarding your financial security.

The next section is for the finance types among you who want to understand how financial planners arrive at this rule of thumb.

If you have little interest in the details, you can skip the next section and move on to "An RRSP Might Not Be Enough."

How Did We Get the 4 to 5 Percent Withdrawal Rate?

There are two very different ways financial analysts have come to the 4+ percent withdrawal rate recommendation: *deterministic analysis* using actual historical rates of return and assuming that history is relevant to the future performance of markets; and stochastic or *Monte Carlo analysis,* which assesses a randomly generated number of total return patterns based on an assumption regarding the type of probability distribution, which is valid only to the extent that this assumption correctly patterns the future distribution of market returns.

Deterministic Analysis: History Is Your Guide

William Bengen, a well-known certified financial planner who is an MIT-trained mathematician and engineer with a master's degree in financial planning, has used historical data on the returns of U.S. stocks, bonds, and Treasury bills since 1926 to study portfolio longevity. Given the actual *total returns* (the sum of capital growth and income) from 1926 until 2004, Bengen calculated the *maximum initial withdrawal rate* that would assure portfolio longevity over a 30-year retirement period for a hypothetical retiree who stopped working in each of the years from 1926 to 1974 (30 years prior to 2004, the last year for which he had data).

Bengen found that the optimal asset mix in a retirement portfolio was around 50 percent stocks and 50 percent bonds.

This flies in the face of conventional wisdom that suggests the closer you get to retirement the larger the bond component should be in your portfolio. Given today's low level of bond yields, *it is essential to hold 45 to 65 percent of your portfolio in stocks* to raise the prospects of the portfolio lasting for 30 years or longer. In general, the maximum safe initial withdrawal rate is about 4.2 percent, rising each year by the rate of inflation.

Stock allocation is especially important if some of your retirement money is in a taxable account. The tax rate on withdrawals from taxable (non-registered) accounts can be lower than the ordinary income tax rate charged on all withdrawals from tax-deferred accounts (RRSPs) because of the lower tax rates on dividends and capital gains. However, the dividends and interest in the taxable account cannot accumulate tax-free. The withdrawal rate rises by 3 percent each year to account for inflation. The value of the portfolio gradually declines until it is nearly exhausted in Year 30. With this methodology, the real purchasing power of retirement income is stabilized. A surge in inflation would likely lead to higher interest rates and stock returns, at least for many stocks, so you would probably be covered with the initial withdrawal rate of about 4.2 percent.

If you want to leave a legacy beyond the value of your home and other illiquid assets, then your initial withdrawal rate would need to be lower (or your nest egg bigger with the same withdrawal rate). Similarly, the *longer* the time horizon in retirement, the *lower* the safe initial withdrawal rate will be, and vice versa. So if you work until age 75, your horizon could be only 20 years. Your peak initial withdrawal rate in this case would be 5.4 percent at only a 30 percent equity allocation. For a 10-year horizon, the safe peak rate is a whopping 8.9 percent with a 40 percent equity allocation rate.

In summary, assuming it is valid that historical investment returns foreshadow the returns of the future, even the longest-lived retirees can safely employ a 4 percent initial withdrawal rate for their portfolios without risk of running out of money.[1]

At a 5 percent initial withdrawal rate, which is commonly recommended today, the certainty of not outliving your money for a 30-year retirement is about 94 percent in a tax-advantaged account made up of 40 percent large-cap stocks, 20 percent small-cap, and 40 percent intermediate-term bonds. Many people see this as a good bet, which is why you often hear that your initial withdrawal rate could safely be 5 percent.[2]

Bengen's historical analysis also showed that during the wealth-accumulation years—say, 35 or 40 years of contributing to a tax-advantaged account—the best historical strategy is to *maintain a 100 percent equity allocation right up until the day you stop working.*[3] A diversified portfolio of high-quality dividend-paying stocks, like the ones I showed you in our stock screen, would be particularly attractive.

Monte Carlo Simulation: A Stochastic Approach

No one knows just how well history can predict the next 30 years or more, particularly given the dramatic structural changes in the global economy. Deterministic analysis uses a rear-view mirror rather than a crystal ball to predict the future, and so does not account well for any prospective "this-time-is-different" developments.

The uncertainty of the level and pattern of annual rates of return over an indeterminate time frame creates risk. This risk has been analyzed with what is called a Monte Carlo simulation.[4] It was named for Monte Carlo, Monaco, where the primary attractions are the roulette wheels, dice, and slot machines of the casinos, all of which exhibit random behaviour.

The random behaviour in games of chance is similar to how Monte Carlo simulation selects variable values at random, within certain pre-specified limits, to simulate a particular set of circumstances (a model). When you roll a die, you know that a 1, 2, 3, 4, 5, or 6 will come up, but you don't know which it will be.

Similarly, we cannot accurately predict the rate of return on our investments or the inflation rate. Consider the following simple example:

> You have $1,000 invested and you expect a 5 percent average yearly return on your investment. In two years, if the annual return is a stable 5 percent each year, your investment will be worth $1,102.50.
>
> Now let's assume your same $1,000 returns minus 5 percent the first year and plus 15 percent the second. Your investment after those two years is worth only $1,092.50, even though your investment returned "on average" 5 percent.

So if you run into a string of bad years early in your retirement, the probability of running out of money is higher.

Monte Carlo analysis is able to estimate the probability of achieving your financial goal by accounting for the yearly variability in the main factors contributing to its outcome. A very large number of trials allows us to compute the statistical probability that your financial plan will be successful. For example, if after 1,000 trials, 750 of those trials achieved your financial goals, your financial plan success rate is 75 percent.

Using this method, financial planners can tell you what the annual withdrawal rate from your portfolio should be to generate a particular probability of achieving your income goal in retirement for all the years that you live. The greater the assurance you need (or the higher the probability of meeting your goal), the smaller the withdrawal rate and/or the larger the required size of your retirement nest egg (the higher the nest egg multiple of the income goal).

Unfortunately, nothing is certain in life, not even death (when?) and taxes (at what rate?). There are problems with the Monte Carlo method, just as there are with the method based solely on historical data. Most importantly, we do not know the probability distribution of stock and bond market returns.[5] Until even more sophisticated techniques are available, *it pays to be conservative in your assumptions.*

> **ANOTHER RULE OF THUMB:** An initial withdrawal rate of 4 to 5 percent is prudent. Keep at least half your portfolio of investible funds in stocks.

An RRSP Might Not Be Enough

Only two-thirds of eligible Canadian households have an RRSP, and only one-third max out their contributions. As of 2005, there was an estimated $406 billion of RRSP contribution room available, which can be used in later years.

Some rough calculations suggest that for many high-income earners, even contributing the maximum allowable to an RRSP (or a 401(k)) each year might not yield a big enough income to maintain your standard of living.

As an example, for a person who is age 50, has no DB employ-ment pension, and has maxed out his or her RRSP contributions for 25 years, the value of the resulting RRSP would be about $700,000. This is assuming that the RRSP funds were invested in a balanced portfolio, with 50 percent in equities, 40 percent in bonds, and 10 percent in cash. While people in this hypothetical situation may still work another 15 years or more, high-income earners would be financially pressed in retirement, because the prudent withdrawal rate of 4 to 5 percent from this RRSP would generate only $28,000 to $35,000 in pre-tax real annual income at today's RRSP level. The CPP top-up would be only about $10,000 (in today's dollars). If you found yourself in this situation, it would likely be a good idea for you to continue working and to save in a non-registered account while still maxing out your RRSP contributions. The taxable account should be fully invested in stocks—high-quality dividend-paying stocks that would meet a dividend stock screen similar to the example in Chapter 8 should be considered, as well as other investments recommended by a trusted qualified investment adviser who understands your particular financial situation and its outlook as well as your risk tolerance and time horizon.

People hit the maximum RRSP contribution of 18 percent of earned income to a maximum of $19,000 in 2007 (less any pension adjustment, plus any carry forward of unused contribu-tions), at an income level of just over $105,500 per year. Assuming this hypothetical 50-year-old earns an average $200,000 annual income in the last five years of working, it would take a $2.8 million to $3.5 million portfolio (in today's dollars) to replace with a high degree of certainty 75 percent of that pre-tax income excluding government pensions.

It's a good thing that maximum RRSP contribution limits are increasing to $20,000 in 2008, and an additional $1,000 per year until it is indexed to average wage growth in 2011 and beyond. If anything, those contribution limits will be raised further by future governments with boomers in mind, given that we are such an important voting bloc. There is also a real issue of fairness and even-handedness in light of the generosity of public sector pensions.

For 60-year-olds today who maxed out their RRSP contributions for the past 35 years, under the same balanced investment assumptions the account would be worth a sizeable $1.3 million. This can prudently generate a pre-tax annual real retirement income of $52,000 to $65,000. Whether that will be enough depends on pre-retirement annual employment income, other pensions, and retirement lifestyle.

The bottom line is that many affluent households will need investible assets in addition to an RRSP to maintain their living standards. Relying too much on equity in your home is risky. If we all rely on selling or refinancing our homes, values will inevitably decline. The amount any bank will offer in a reverse mortgage depends on the assessed market value of your home. Immediate fixed annuities that pay lifetime income are expensive. At today's rates, an annuity for a 60-year-old that generates $50,000 pre-tax annual income would cost roughly $700,000 to $800,000 (depending on whether it is for a male or female, with the male's annuity less expensive due to his shorter actuarial life expectancy). As we discussed in Chapter 7, you are not allowed to borrow more than 10 to 40 percent of the appraised value of your house, so, in this example, a reverse mortgage would generate nowhere near enough income. Most people don't like reverse mortgages or plain-vanilla annuities anyway, because if you die prematurely, you won't get your money's worth. You can buy annuities that have a death benefit, but they are even more expensive.[6]

Why 15 Percent Is the New 10 Percent

For years we have been told that if we save 10 percent of our before-tax income (including any employer pension or non-pension savings contributions) we will be primed for a long and secure retirement. Too many people barely save at all, but many who have followed the 10 percent rule will discover they have to delay their retirement because they still don't have enough money. After thousands of simulations, financial-services company T. Rowe Price in Baltimore, Maryland, determined that the old rule no longer works. It counsels that by saving at least 15 percent of your salary (plus bonus or any other monetary compensation), and investing 60 percent of it in stocks and 40 percent in bonds, you will replace about 50 percent of pre-retirement income before factoring in Social Security (or CPP) and any pension. We saw earlier that financial planner William Bengen would recommend investing the 15 percent of your gross income in an equity-only portfolio.

There are some stipulations here: The calculations assume you have been saving 15 percent from day one of your career. But if, for instance, you are 20 years away from retirement and have saved little to this point, you'll need to sock away 25 percent of every paycheque to replace only 34 percent of pre-retirement income before government pension is included. This 15 percent rate does include any employer contributions to your RRSP, 401(k), or other retirement account. Now you can see how valuable a DB pension is.

This relates to our retirement arithmetic as follows. Assume that you work for 40 years. Wages during your working years grow at a constant 2.5 percent per year. Saving 10 percent of your income each year of your working life assures a nest egg equal to 10 times your working-life average annual income, assuming average annual real (after inflation) total returns of 4.7 percent. If you assume an average annual real total return of a more prudent 4 percent, saving 10 percent of your income would give you a nest egg of 8.6 times your average working-life income, or most likely 5.8 times the average income of your last five years. This replaces 29 percent of your final five-year average annual earnings, assuming a 5 percent withdrawal rate. In addition, you would earn your government pension and any private pension you are entitled to.

If, instead of a 4 percent real return per year, we had assumed 5 percent, you would have replaced 36 percent of your final five-year annual earnings rather than 29 percent. Presumably you would be taking more risk to garner the additional percentage point in return, although that really depends on the vagaries of the markets going forward, as well as your asset mix—the more stocks relative to bonds, the higher the likely average real return.

Now let's look at the 15 percent savings rate. Again assuming an average total real return of 4 percent a year, saving 15 percent per year would generate a nest egg of 13 times your total working-life average annual income, or roughly 8.8 times the average income in your last five years of work under the same assumptions we used in the 10 percent example. This would generate an annual retirement income of 44 percent of your final five-year average earnings plus any government or other pension earnings. Assuming a real annual return on your portfolio of 5 percent—rather than 4 percent—which is reasonable, your annual retirement income from your portfolio would amount to 54 percent of your average earnings in the last five years you work.

These retirement incomes might still be a bit skinny, depending on your lifestyle and your other retirement income. But remember, the last 10 years of your working life should be your maximum wealth-accumulation years. Your actual living expenses are probably going to be well below your average earnings during those years, as you likely will have paid down much of your debt, finished with tuition payments, and finally got your kids off the payroll. Of course, circumstances differ among households. Some will be helping dependent parents. Some will have children later in life and therefore will be covering university costs well into their late 50s or even 60s (think of those men who have a second family with a wife who is 20 years younger).

Another way to improve your financial position in retirement is to work longer. Assume again that you save 10 percent of your income each year at a 4 percent real rate of return. Retiring at age 65 allows you to replace 29 percent of the average income of your last five years. Now, consider working an extra five years and retiring at age 70. In this case, assuming income continues to grow at 2.5 percent per year, you would generate a nest egg that is about one-third larger than the one you would have if you were to stop working at age 65. This nest egg will replace 34 percent of the (now higher) income of your last five years of work, or 39 percent of your five-year income had you retired at age 65. If increasing your savings rate from 10 percent to 15 percent is not feasible, a few additional years of work can have a similar positive impact on your retirement nest egg—not to mention the increased government pension benefits you will receive by waiting until age 70 to begin your CPP payments (62 percent greater than if you'd taken the money at age 60).

Assuming a real return of 5 percent per year, if you saved 10 percent of your income, you would replace 36 percent of your final five-year average income. And working an additional five years you would generate a nest egg that is one-third larger (same as in the 4 percent–return example) and able to replace roughly 44 percent of your now higher income of the last five years of work or 49 percent of your five-year income had you retired at age 65. Additionally, working to just past your 71st birthday with a 10 percent savings rate would provide a nest egg equivalent to the one you would obtain by saving 15 percent per year until age 65.

These examples are merely meant to illustrate just how saving a larger percentage of your income, working longer, or earning a higher rate of return can affect your retirement security. Here is a list of the examples that show clearly that working longer (not just from age 65 to age 70, but from 55 to 60, or 50 to 55) can have a dramatic impact on the value of your nest egg—so does saving more, even if only for the last few years of your work life.[7]

Total Real Return of 4 Percent Per Year

saving 15 percent (working to 65) = 1.5 x saving 10 percent (working to 65)

working to 70 (saving 10 percent) = 1.32 x working to 65 (saving 10 percent)

working to 65 (saving 15 percent) = working to 73.5 (saving 10 percent)

Total Return of 5 Percent Per Year

saving 15 percent (working to 65) = 1.5 x saving 10 percent (working to 65)

working to 70 (saving 10 percent) = 1.36 x working to 65 (saving 10 percent)

working to 65 (saving 15 percent) = working to 71.5 (saving 10 percent)

From this we can see that you can trade off a lower savings rate for a few more years of work and get the additional benefits of a higher average income level for the years over age 65, higher government pension payments for the remaining years of life, and fewer years to depend on your portfolio. This reduces your needed portfolio longevity, which means that your initial safe withdrawal rate can be higher, generating more income in retirement.

Ways to Stretch Those Retirement Savings Dollars

These nest egg numbers can still seem daunting. But as I mentioned earlier, your spending requirements in retirement will be lower than when you worked full time. Work-related expenses, the amount of money you had to save for retirement, and contributions to Employment Insurance and CPP (or Social Security) are no longer required. You are likely to need less in the way of domestic help, at least in the early-retirement years, and with a less hectic life you could eat out less often. All of the conveniences you needed to maintain a very tight work/family schedule could be reduced if not eliminated. Therefore to maintain your living standards you might need only 60 to 70 percent of your maximum employment income.

What else can you do to dial down your *unfunded retirement liability?* To squeeze more income out of your assets, you might consider a reverse mortgage and/or use 25 to 50 percent of your savings to buy a fixed annuity that pays lifetime income. This wouldn't be my preference, because both are very costly, and if you die relatively young, you've "spent" a lot of money that could have gone to your heirs or to charity. Reverse mortgages and traditional annuities are expensive and if you die soon after you have chosen either of these options, they could be very costly.

But there are other ways. You could try to cut your spending, and therefore income requirements, by reducing your fixed costs. A smaller house would lower your property taxes, lower your utilities expenses, and leave you more money to put into your portfolio. You could also move to a cheaper locale, farther, for example, from the city centre, which might not matter when you don't go to work downtown each day, or even to a smaller town, where costs of living are generally lower. There are many resources available specifically for retirees to help you choose where to move based on your particular wants and needs. You may have a preference for a hot and steamy climate or desert dry, a university town or farming community, ski hills or ocean-front, or you may want to put the emphasis on cultural, sports, or medical facilities, and so on. You might also want to reassess how many cars you need. Deciding how and where to live and what extras you can reasonably do without sure isn't easy and you might try to downscale before you stop working to see how palatable it is. If you've got problems with it, you might want to retire a little later, or phase in your retirement, working part time for a number of years.

As we have seen, postponing retirement can make a big differ-ence. It gives you more time to save and more time for your investments to pay off. It will also shorten your retirement so you can be more aggressive in spending your nest egg. An added benefit of working longer is that you can postpone taking CPP or Social Security and purchasing an annuity. The result would be that when you start your government pension and buy your annuity, you will get even more income.

There is also a typical pattern in your retirement years: Often your travel expenses go up in early retirement, but by the time you are 75 or so you will likely be less inclined to travel as much, or play golf or ski as much. Studies show that people do tend to spend less later in retirement. Folks aged 75 and older typically spend 10 percent less per person than those 65 to 74. The reality is, however, that most retirees do not have much financial room to manoeuvre, and if they are spending less after age 75, it is often because they have no choice. Inflation for seniors in the United States may be higher than it is for the general population because of the outsized rise in the price of medicine and health-care services.

For more affluent retirees, however, the slowdown in spending as the years progress might well be voluntary. Much of their income may have gone toward travel, eating out, and other extravagances in the early "go-go" years, but in the subsequent "go-slow" years they might be less inclined to spend at the same rate. In the late "no-go" years, expenses could soar with home-care or nursing-home costs, and you could live a surprisingly long time.[8]

Two-Stage Retirement

Another option is to think of your retirement in two stages: the period before age 85 and the period after. Let's say you retire at age 65. You could live on about 85 percent of your retirement nest egg for 20 years, which would allow you to begin with a withdrawal rate of about 5.4 percent with only about one-third of your assets in stocks. You can adjust this as the years progress depending on your portfolio performance. The withdrawal rate would rise with the rate of inflation each year. This would give you far more income than would the traditional approach of an initial withdrawal rate of just over 4 percent.

The other 15 percent of your nest egg could be invested in a mix of stocks and 20-year Canadian government real return bonds, or inflation-indexed U.S. Treasury bonds, depending on where you will be spending most of your time (Canada or the United States). If you are still alive at age 85, you can spend down this money gradually or use it to buy an income annuity, which is relatively inexpensive at that age because the insurance companies know they are unlikely to pay out for more than a decade or so, and maybe far less.[9] If necessary, you could supplement this income with a conventional or reverse mortgage. This is not ideal for those who want to leave a large bequest, but if you're short on savings you will stretch your retirement nest egg with a higher income. If you die before age 85, your heirs will inherit a decent sum, and if you live longer you should be reasonably comfortable.

KEY POINTS

- With the help of a financial planner, estimate the pre-tax income you will need in retirement over and above your income from government and private pensions and other sources.

- As a rule of thumb, you will need a retirement nest egg of between 20 and 25 times the level of this additional desired pre-tax annual income to generate the income you need.

- This is a conservative rule, allowing you to withdraw between 4 and 5 percent of your nest egg in your first year of retirement. Each subsequent year, you can increase your withdrawal rate by the rate of inflation.

- There are many factors that affect this rule of thumb and your nest egg multiple. Whatever the multiple, the withdrawal rate is 1 divided by that number. For example, a multiple of 20 bears a withdrawal rate of 5 percent. A multiple of 25 is associated with an initial withdrawal rate of 4 percent. The higher the multiple, the lower the withdrawal rate, and the more conservative you are being.

- Multiples rise and withdrawal rates fall: the longer the retirement period (the longer you live in retirement); the more conservative your rate of return assumption; the more money you want to leave to your heirs; or the more certain you want to be that you will not run out of money.

- Given today's low level of bond yields, it is essential to hold 45 to 65 percent of your portfolio in stocks during retirement to increase the prospects of the portfolio lasting for 30 years or longer.

- Stock allocation is especially important if some of your retirement money is in a taxable account. The tax rate on withdrawals from taxable (non-registered) accounts can be lower than the ordinary income tax rate charged on all withdrawals from tax-deferred accounts (RRSPs) because of the lower tax rates on dividends and capital gains.

- At a 5 percent initial withdrawal rate (equivalent to a nest egg multiple of 20), which is commonly recommended today, the certainty of not outliving your money for a 30-year retirement is about 94 percent if your investment portfolio consists of 40 percent large-cap stocks, 20 percent small-cap, and 40 percent interme-diate-term bonds. Many people see this as a good bet, which is why you often hear that your initial withdrawal rate could safely be 5 percent.

- For many affluent households, savings beyond an RRSP might be necessary because of the contribution limits.

- You can trade off a lower savings rate for a few more years of work and get the additional benefits of a higher average income level for the years working over age 65, higher government pension payments for the remaining years of life, and fewer years to depend on your portfolio. This reduces your needed portfolio longevity, which means that your initial safe withdrawal rate can therefore be higher, generating more income in retirement.

- It may not be enough to save 10 percent of your pre-tax income. Many won't meet their retirement goals unless they save 15 percent of their gross income or work a few years beyond age 65, depending on how large their other sources of income are.

- The nest egg sums required to live comfortably in retirement might be out of reach for some boomers, particularly those relatively close to retirement. There are ways to stretch your retirement nest egg: cut overhead costs; plan to spend more in the first decade of retirement and less thereafter; plan your retirement income flow in two stages by setting aside 85 percent of your nest egg, invested in stocks and bonds, to cover your needs until age 85. The remaining 15 percent should be invested in high-quality stocks and real return bonds, which are indexed to the rate of inflation. Assuming you retire at 65, your initial withdrawal rate from the larger portion of your nest egg could be 5.4 percent, rising each year with the rate of inflation. If you live to be 85, you can live off the remaining portion of your nest egg or use it to buy an annuity, which will be relatively inexpensive at that age.

Chapter 10

Health and Happiness in Act III

A successful retirement for most people—be it at age 55, 65, or 75—is to be physically and fiscally independent, to be active, and to have love and purpose in their lives. My own interest led me to do some reading on the subject of later-life happiness. Our society is fixated on the maintenance of youth, and most boomers have fallen into that trap, which only makes aging seem all the more difficult and depressing. Other cultures have revered the wisdom and experience of the aged, but certainly not ours. That will be changing as role models of a happy productive later life increasingly abound and as boomers contemplate Act III of their own lives.

Boomers are "retiring" retirement as our parents' generation knew it. We will not settle for personal diminishment, social isolation, dependency, and inertia. In mind and body we will remain active for as long as possible, and most of us will continue to be productive well into our eighth decade. Our later years will be more vital and exhilarating than they were for any previous generation, as we are the healthiest and wealthiest generation ever to retire. And we can learn to age well, through a growing body of scientific research that now suggests a number of predictive elements and learned behaviours that can add healthy, productive years to our lives.

Aging Well

As the older boomers approach later life, gerontology, the scientific study of the biological, psychological, and sociological phenomena associated with old age and aging, is getting increased attention. Long-term clinical research suggests there are some key attitudes and abilities, many of them learned, that assist in aging well. There are also benefits to the maturing process, as stress diminishes and most people re-evaluate what is important in life. The impulse to be ostentatious and competitive typically wanes; the wise ones are more comfortable in their skin than ever before, and there is time to experience the beauty in the world and to nurture younger people and each other. Healthy older brains are better at dealing with complex situations, having the benefit of so much experience. Emotions can be more easily controlled, and the opportunity to feel joy and have peace of mind is greater than at any other time in our lives. These studies suggest that people who have aged well wouldn't want to go back to their childhood, teens, or young adulthood, or the rat race years of career achievement in their 40s and 50s. Many are quite content to be right where they are in the life cycle. With advances in our knowledge about the aging process, many experts now believe there is no reason to suffer enormous and prolonged pain, degeneration, and inactivity before death.

One of the world's longest continuous studies of human physical and mental health has followed 237 students at Harvard

University and 332 socially disadvantaged youths from inner-city Boston since 1937 through health, illness, and death. Dr. George Vaillant, professor of psychiatry at Harvard Medical School, directed the study and has shown that *successful aging* is not an oxymoron. Dr. Vaillant believes that "you can add life to your years instead of just years to your life."[1]

Vaillant and his colleagues discovered predictors of how well an individual in mid-life is likely to age. Some of these have been known for some time. For example, substance abuse of any kind—tobacco, drugs, alcohol, even excessive junk food—continuing into your 40s and 50s will markedly increase your chances of chronic disease and premature death. Another familiar leading indicator and contributor to healthful aging is a stable happy marriage. Whether this is the cause of happiness and wellness or the result of it, we can't say, but it clearly makes a big difference, especially for men, who often leave the task of developing and maintaining a social network to their partners. The deep social connection of a good marriage is estimated to add one and a half to three years to a man's life and a half a year to a woman's. The benefit is thought to be smaller for women because they tend to have a much broader, diverse network of contacts on their own.[2]

For those who have lost their partner, critically important are good friends and even a pet. Many studies find that older people with pets feel needed and loved; they are more content and healthier. Social contact is also crucial, especially having one or two very close friends; it is also of great value to spend time with younger people on a regular basis.

In addition, Vaillant and his colleagues found that education is positively correlated to happiness and health later in life. In fact, perhaps surprisingly, *education trumps money and social prestige as a route to happiness and health.* "Despite great differences in parental social class, college-tested intelligence, current income, and job status, the health decline of the 25 inner-city men who obtained a college education was no more rapid than of the Harvard College graduates," Vaillant pointed out.[3]

Similarly, those who enjoy reading are also likely to be more content and active. Continued brain work—be it through reading or writing, attending lectures or taking classes, playing bridge or chess, or doing crossword or Sudoku puzzles—exercises the brain and makes it more resilient. It also strengthens the immune system. So does walking, swimming, and other forms of light exercise. Moreover, mental and physical exercise increases those feel-good hormones, endorphins, as well as neurotransmitters such as serotonin. Endorphins reduce the sensation of pain and affect emotions in a positive way. Increased levels of serotonin tend to elevate mood and prevent depression. As well, exercise is a key contributor to weight management.

Attitude Creates Latitude

Mature defences or an *active-coping style* may be most important of all. As Charles Darwin realized, it is not the size or strength of a species that assures its endurance, but its adaptability to changing forces. Life is full of changes, and some of them are unpleasant or downright terrible. The capacity to adapt and to endure frustration and loss is essential to successful aging. Good coping or adapting skills get us through the harder times sustaining less of the damage caused by stress, anger, resentment, or depression. Key to these skills is a positive attitude, outside interests, sociability, and the ability to play, as well as a sense of humour, altruism (giving of yourself to others), anticipation, and joie de vivre.[4]

Also playing a role are sublimation and suppression. *Sublimation* is the act of diverting the energy associated with an unacceptable impulse or drive (such as rage or despair) into a personally and socially acceptable activity—turning lemons into lemonade. Sublimation finds the silver lining in a painful or undesirable experience. *Suppression* (keeping a stiff upper lip) is the act of temporarily postponing or ignoring a desire when unavoidable circumstances stand in the way; but the desire and the hope of realizing it are not forgotten. Suppression is not the same as the unhealthy response of *repression,* which is the act of burying and forgoing the desire or the gratification of achieving new goals or satisfying new wants and longings.

Mature coping mechanisms lead to emotional well-being and satisfaction. They are the most adaptive responses and require the least amount of energy.

Immature defences, on the other hand, produce sad results. Don't blame others for your problems or deny that you have problems. Don't harbour resentment or anger; it will only corrode your body and destroy your peace of mind. Having false rather than real friends can cause more problems than it solves. So does distracting yourself by sipping scotch, overeating, and watching too much television. These are methods of self-medication that temporarily mask the problem while it continues to fester. Self-medication through drugs, if unmonitored by a physician, is the same whether the drugs are illicit or prescription.

There is a great deal of misunderstanding and misinformation about some medications, particularly antidepressants. These are not "happy pills," as some people suggest. They are not equivalent to the temporary relief attained from alcohol or some illicit drugs. Antidepressants, when appropriately administered and monitored, can be wonderful in the treatment of clinical depression caused by the ineffective functioning of neurotransmitters in the brain. They come with risks as well as benefits. But when used under a doctor's supervision, they can create normal brain function. This is not drug abuse and can add "life to your years and years to your life" at any age. Recent studies show that untreated clinical depression is very negative for brain and body health; it seems to be associated with a higher incidence of Alzheimer's disease and even cancer, cardiac problems, and overeating.

There are two fundamental tasks to healthy maturation:

- to become a secure individual in what you view as a neutral world
- to develop an unshakeable sense of self-worth—of who you are—which goes well beyond what you do for a living

A sense of self-worth, and the view that the world is neutral rather than treacherous and hostile, allows us to bounce back after the trials that life occasionally throws at us. Bad things happen—things that challenge our sense of ourselves—often inexplicably and without warning. Most of us have suffered blows that have shaken us to the core, leading us to at least temporarily question our self-worth. Be it a job termination, a personal rejection of any sort, the loss of a loved one, public failure or humiliation, or being passed over for a promotion, it hits hard, emotionally and cognitively. But an inability to let go of the pain and put it behind us without prolonged anger or resentment is not healthy. Those who can reasonably quickly see such events as challenges, and see challenges as opportunities, will age far better than those who believe the person, the company, or the world is rotten.

The seven controllable predictors of late-life happiness are:

- responsible drinking
- no smoking
- relationship stability
- education
- exercise
- weight control
- mature coping skills

Adherence to these predictions before age 50 can contribute to good physical and mental health at ages 70, 80, and older.

Uncontrollable factors that affect successful aging include parents' social class, family cohesion, longevity of ancestors, and childhood temperament. However, by age 70 these factors are no longer important. High cholesterol before age 50, for example, also loses importance after your 70th birthday. *However, good physical health at age 50 (a plus) and major depression (a minus) remain important throughout life.* Dr. Vaillant researched predictors of successful aging in women as well and found no difference.[5]

As we get older, maintenance becomes more important than genes. It appears that the key to a successful later life may be found not so much in our genetic destiny as in ourselves.

Optimism

According to most psychologists, learned optimism and *self-efficacy* lead to mental health. There is a distinction between self-esteem and self-efficacy. Self-esteem relates to your sense of self-worth, whereas self-efficacy relates to your perception of your ability to reach a goal. A mentally healthy person goes through life with the following internal belief: "The good things that happen to me will last forever. They are pervasive, and they are my own doing. The bad things that happen to me occur by chance, are limited, and are unlikely to happen again."[6]

Optimism permits us to contemplate and plan for the future, rather than deny or dread it. Studies have repeatedly shown "future-mindedness" to be a critical ingredient of mature mental health. But you aren't born with this mindset, you develop it. Psychologists tell us that adult mental health represents a "continuing process of maturational unfolding";[7] we are never too old to learn, and under normal circumstances we can continue to learn nearly as long as we live. Research shows that in the absence of disease the brain works well at least until age 80,[8] and that, neurologically, optimal brain development requires almost a lifetime.[9] Studies reveal that healthy individuals are less depressed and show greater emotional modulation at 70 than they did at 30.[10] We really aren't just getting older, we are getting better—just like good red wine.

The Maturation Process

Erik Erikson, a German-born American psychoanalyst and educator whose studies in the 1950s have perhaps contributed most to the understanding of psychosocial development, provided one of the first models of adult social development. His model was later augmented and refined by George Vaillant and others. Their work conceptualized human development as expanding ripples in a pond (Chart 30). Erikson believed that our personality develops in accordance with our ability and desire to widen our "social radius"—the circle of people with whom we interact. He thought that this requires the sequential movement through six developmental stages, but later research suggests that these stages are not necessarily sequential; they can each occur at different and multiple times in our lives and they don't necessarily occur in the order Erikson posited or even at all. The theory, however, is widely accepted as a useful framework or map for identifying and understanding unresolved issues or conflicts and their impact on our behaviour, emotion, and cognition—and thus our ability to age well.

The model is suggestive of what it takes ultimately to achieve satisfying maturation, regardless of when and in which order these developments occur. Many successful people in one realm miss one or even two of these stages in another realm, but the

Chart 30

Erikson-Vaillant Model of Adult Development

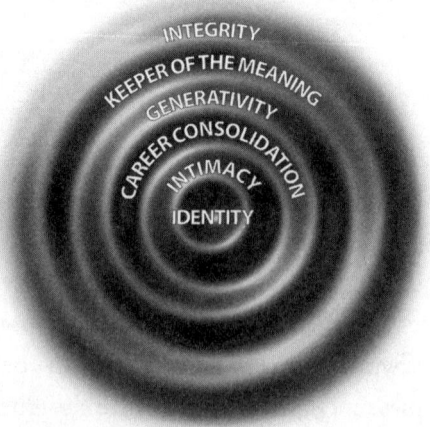

Source: George E. Vaillant, "Mental Health," *American Journal of Psychiatry* 160 (2003). Reprinted with permission.

likelihood of health and happiness throughout life, and especially in late life, improves with the achievement of all of these developmental levels. The six stages include the following: developing a personal identity and autonomy apart from your parents and family; learning to live in a committed, interdependent, mutually happy relationship for many years, thereby choosing intimacy over isolation; career consolation, which requires not only a job, but contentment, reward, competence, commitment, and growth in your job(s).

The fourth stage, called *generativity,* is the unselfish caring for and guiding of the next generation—giving back to society. Current research suggests that some time between ages 35 and 60 our need for personal achievement usually wanes and our need for community involvement waxes. This might sound odd to a busy 30- or 40-something who is raising a family and striving to get that next promotion; but judging from what I see, it does happen. Generativity is reflected in community service, fundraising, teaching, consulting, and mentoring or coaching. It can also be performing socially valued work or public service, or having protégés, apprentices, or disciples. It reflects the capacity to give of yourself and to accomplish something of meaning. The alternative is stagnation. The better you are at generativity, the happier you are likely to be as you grow older. It will be easier to adjust to the inevitable losses of aging if you can relate and bond with people beyond your immediate family and long-standing circle of friends, finding a purpose at any stage of life.

Another important developmental stage is to become what psychologists call a *keeper of the meaning.* Like grandparenthood, this involves passing on the traditions of the past to the future. The focus is on conservation and preservation of the culture, community, and environment, rather than just the development of its children. Grandparents and others of the same generation are usually better at this than 30-year-olds, but it can occur earlier in life.

In the final stage of development, which can occur for some people long before old age, you come to the realization that you are part of something greater than your immediate social radius. This stage they called *integrity*, not just in the sense of a steadfast adherence to a moral or ethical code, but also the quality of being whole or undivided—completeness without duplicity. This is the state of achieving some sense of peace and unity with your own life. Your social radius could expand to embrace the whole world if you have the capacity to think and engage on a global basis— as it clearly already has for Bill and Melinda Gates or Bill Clinton—but for most of us it is the ability to give of ourselves beyond our own milieu. Erikson described integrity as an experience that conveys some world order and sense of spirituality.

The Bottom Line

I know we've strayed a long way from the subject of financial planning and the other traditional topics of retirement books, especially those written by a financial type like me. But while my intellectual journey through my own transitioning to later life began with planning my financial future, it quickly covered wider ground. How could I imagine what I would need financially if I didn't know where I was headed in terms of lifestyle, health, goals, and development? This soon led me to ponder how I could make a difference, and what kind of legacy I would like to leave for my family, my friends, my community, and the world.

Being who I am, I like to think about these very personal issues in the context of the global economic and financial future, a context that comes very naturally to me. Much of my professional life involves forecasting, hence my desire to plan. What isn't easy is deciding what I want, how I ideally see my own Act III, and how to maximize my chances of realizing my intentions. Much of what I have written in this book originated from my own personal planning. No doubt other boomers are also pondering the same issues or will be before too long.

It became clear to me as this process evolved that there was so much more to this than just financial security, as important as that is. It is a necessary, but not sufficient, condition (as we economists say) for the happy, healthy, independent, and productive later life to which I look forward. So I studied far afield from economics and financial planning, and in areas in which I claim no expertise. But these are issues we all need to think about, at least implicitly, in creating that financial plan.

I am now more convinced than ever that life does actually get better and better. And as much as I have generally enjoyed all of the stages to this point, I believe the best is yet to come.

KEY POINTS

- A successful retirement for most people is to be physically and fiscally independent, to be active, and to have love and purpose in their lives.

- In the new retirement we will not settle for personal diminishment, social isolation, dependency, and inertia. We will remain active in mind and body, and most of us will continue to be productive well into our eighth decade.

- We can learn to age well through a growing body of scientific research that now suggests a number of predictive elements and learned behaviours can add healthy productive years to our lives.

- There are benefits to the maturing process, as stress diminishes and most people re-evaluate what is important in life.

- Healthy older brains are better at dealing with complex situations that you have dealt with for many years, having the benefit of so much experience. Emotions can be more easily controlled, and the opportunity to feel joy and have peace of mind is greater than at any other time in our lives.

- Research suggests certain predictors of how well an individual in mid-life is likely to age. These include no substance abuse (including cigarettes); a good, stable marriage; education and ongoing reading; brain work; exercise; normal body weight; and a positive attitude. Mid-lifers who exhibit these characteristics have a greater likelihood of aging well.

- Education trumps money and social prestige as a route to happiness and health. Education is more than a degree earned 40 years ago; it is an ongoing interest in the world around you, reading newspapers, books, and other sources of information and awareness. Those who love to read fall into this category. And you don't have to read only non-fiction; good fiction can also be enlightening as well as entertaining.

- A positive attitude is much more than being unrealistically optimistic. The reality is that bad things will happen to all of us.

- Good coping or adapting skills are essential to successful aging. So is the ability to endure frustration.

- Key to these skills is a positive attitude, a sense of humour, altruism, anticipation, outside interests, sociability, sublimation (turning lemons into lemonade), suppression (keeping a stiff upper lip), and the ability to play.

- Uncontrollable factors that affect successful aging include parents' social class, family cohesion, longevity of ancestors, and childhood temperament. However, by age 70, these factors are no longer important.

- We are never too old to learn, and under normal circumstances we can continue to learn nearly as long as we live. Adult mental health represents a "continuing process of maturational unfolding."

- Neurologically, optimal brain development requires almost a lifetime.

- The likelihood of health and happiness throughout life and especially in late life improves with the achievement of six developmental stages:

  - developing a personal *identity* and autonomy apart from parents and family

  - learning to live in a committed, interdependent, mutually happy relationship for many years (*intimacy* over isolation)

  - *career consolation,* which requires not only a job, but contentment, reward, competence, commitment, and growth in your job(s)

  - *generativity,* which is unselfishly caring for and guiding the next generation—giving back to society

  - becoming a *keeper of the meaning,* which involves passing on the traditions of the past to the future

  - *integrity,* not just in the sense of a steadfast adherence to a moral or ethical code, but also achieving some sense of peace and unity with your own life

Notes

Chapter 1: The New Retirement

1. AXA Retirement Scope, *Retirement: A New Life After Work?* Wave 2, Canadian Results with International Comparisons (Canada: AXA, 2006).

2. BMO Financial Group/Ipsos Reid, *BMO Retirement Trends Study: Presentation to BMO* (Toronto: 2005).

3. Bureau of Labor Statistics, *Monthly Labor Review* (Washington, D.C.: Bureau of Labor Statistics, 2007).

4. Sue Shellenbarger, "More New Mothers Are Staying Home Even When It Causes Financial Pain," *The Wall Street Journal,* November 30, 2006, D1.

Chapter 2: The Generational Divide

1. See Sherry Cooper, *The Cooper Files* (Toronto: Key Porter, 1999), and Sherry Cooper, *Ride the Wave* (Toronto: Financial Times Prentice Hall Canada, 2001) for details.

2. John Sabelhaas and Joyce Manchester, "Baby Boomers and Their Parents: How Does Their Economic Well-Being Compare in Middle Age?" *The Journal of Human Resources* 30, no. 4 (1995): 791–806.

3. The Conference Board of Canada, *The Strategic Value of People: Human Resource Trends and Metrics,* Publication 003-07 (Ottawa: Conference Board of Canada, 2006), 5–17.

4. The dates for this generation vary among commentators. Some have broken this into two generations, creating a dividing line at 1996 (or even 2001). Those born during the earlier period are boomer kids, and those born later are largely the kids of Gen Xers. This distinction (often observed with the use of two terms, Gen Y and Gen Z) is still arbitrary and shifting, so we have put them together under the general rubric of Generation Y, the eldest of whom are the boomer kids, with a relatively small contribution of Gen Xer kids in the past decade or so.

Chapter 3: Health and Achievement: The Keys for Successful Retirement

1. Gina Kolata, "So Big and Healthy Grandpa Wouldn't Even Know You," *The New York Times,* July 30, 2006, www.nytimes.com/2006/07/30/health/30age.html?ei=5070&en=55ee76d6029951f5&ex=1172293200&adxnnl=1&adxnnlx=1172166163-wWmkGIoc4KWOrf8BYGZQMw (July 30, 2006).

2. Statistics Canada, *The Daily: General Social Survey: Social Support and Ageing,* Cat no. 11-001-XIE (Ottawa: Statistics Canada, 2003), 2–3.

3. Gordon B.T. Merman, Richard W. Johnson, and Dan Murphy, "Why Do Boomers Plan to Work So Long?" *The Urban Institute, Discussion Paper,* 06-04 (2006): 3.

4. Claudia Dreifus, "Focusing on the Issue of Aging, and Growing Into the Job," *The New York Times,* November 14, 2006, S2.

5. Gina Kolata, "So Big and Healthy Grandpa Wouldn't Even Know You," *The New York Times,* July 30, 2006, www.nytimes.com/2006/07/30/health/30age.html?ex=1172120400&en=b6bc1636706bc157&ei=5070 (July 30, 2006).

6. The Strategic Counsel, *State of the Baby Boomers: A Report to BMO Financial Group* (Toronto: 2006).

7. P.W. Sullivan, E.H. Morrato, V. Ghushchyan, H.R. Wyatt, and J.O. Hill, "Obesity, Inactivity, and the Prevalence of Diabetes and Diabetes-Related Cardiovascular Comorbidities in the U.S., 2000–2002," *Diabetes Care* 28, no. 7 (2005): 1599–1603.

8. "Obesity" is defined as a body mass index (BMI) of 30 and higher. Your BMI is calculated by dividing your weight in pounds by your height in inches squared, and multiplying that total by 703. Someone who is 5'4" would have to weigh 175 pounds to reach that threshold. (For some people, particularly athletes who exercise a great deal, their BMI could show them as being obese when, in fact, they are in excellent physical condition. Muscle weighs more than fat.) David G. Marrero, "Time to Get Moving: Helping Patients with Diabetes Adopt Exercise as Part of a Healthy Lifestyle," *Clinical Diabetes* 23, no. 4 (2005): 154–59.

9. NAASO: The Obesity Society, "Medical Complications of Obesity," www.obesityonline.org/slides (October 10, 2006).

10. World Health Organization, *Preventing Chronic Diseases: A Vital Investment,* ISBN: 92-4-156300-1 (Geneva: World Health Organization, 2005), 74–83.

11. Dr. Samuel Klein to Dr. Sherry Cooper, personal email, February 19, 2007.

12. Philip T. James, Rachel Leach, Eleni Kalamara, and Maryam Shayeghi, "Section I: Obesity, the Major Health Issue of the 21st Century: The Worldwide Obesity Epidemic," *The North American Association for the Study of Obesity,* www.obesityresearch.org/cgi/content/full/9/suppl_4/S228#F1 (February 19, 2006).

13. Ibid.

14. Roni Rabin, "Health Disparities Persist for Men, and Doctors Ask Why," *The New York Times,* November 14, 2006, www.nytimes.com/2006/11/14/health/14men.html?ex=1321160400&en=1668bbac347e8d5d&ei=5088&partner=rssnyt&emc=rss (November 14, 2006).

15. Stefan Felder, "The Gender Longevity Gap: Explaining the Difference between Singles and Couples," *Journal of Population Economics,* August 2, 2005, www.med.uni-magdeburg.de/fme/institute/ism/Gesoek/felder/gender.pdf (February 8, 2007).

16. Roni Rabin, "Health Disparities Persist for Men, and Doctors Ask Why," *The New York Times,* November 14, 2006, www.nytimes.com/2006/11/14/health/14men.html?ex=1321160400&en=1668bbac347e8d5d&ei=5088&partner=rssnyt&emc=rss (November 14, 2006).

17. Sam Roberts, "51 percent of Women Are Now Living without Spouse," *The New York Times,* January 16, 2007, A1.

18. This section benefits from the valuable expertise of Dr. Elaine Chin, medical director of Scienta Health in Toronto, and naturopath Dr. Shelley Burns, also of Scienta Health.

19. Andy Kessler, *The End of Medicine: How Silicon Valley (and Naked Mice) Will Reboot Your Doctor* (U.S.: HarperCollins, 2006).

20. Dr. Samuel Klein to Dr. Sherry Cooper, personal email, February 15, 2007.

21. Milken Institute DVDs "The Coming American Health Renaissance and the Role of Nutrition," "The Future of Health Care," and "Readying U.S. Health Care for a Time of Healthy Aging and Longer Lives: What We Will Really Need from Our Doctors" (Milken Institute Global Conference, Los Angeles, CA, April 24–26, 2006).

22. "The Wellness Boom," *The Economist,* January 6, 2007, 51.

23. Laura Nash and Howard Stevenson, *Just Enough: Tools for Creating Success in Your Work and Life* (Hoboken, N.J.: John Wiley & Sons, 2004), 15.

24. Ibid., 27.

Chapter 4: Canadian Boomers in a Global Context

1. PRB, "Data Finder," *Population Reference Bureau (PRB) 2006 World Population Data Sheet,* February 8, 2007, www.prb.org/Data Find/datafinder7.htm (February 15, 2007).

2. Ibid.

3. Keith Bradsher, "The Next Industrial Giant Is ... India?" *The New York Times,* August 31, 2006, www.nytimes.com/2006/08/31/business/31cnd-rupee.html?ex=1314676800&en=3d19abd279037 e05&ei=5088&partner=rssnyt&emc=rss (August 31, 2006).

4. Chen Feng, "Official Calls for Criminalization of Sex Identification," *China View: Xinhua online* (in English), May 1, 2006, news.xinhuanet.com/english/2006-05/01/content_4499663.htm (February 15, 2007).

5. Ontario Ministry of Labour, *Pregnancy Leave and Parental Leave,* July 2006, www.labour.gov.on.ca/english/es/factsheets/fs_preg.html (February 15, 2007).

6. Jack M. Mintz, "The 2006 Competitiveness Report: Proposals for Pro-Growth Tax Reform," *C.D. Howe Institute Commentary,* 239 (2006).

7. Ibid., 1.

8. The federal government raised the age from 69 to 71 in the February 2007 budget.

9. PricewaterhouseCoopers, *The 2006 Survey of Canadian Private Companies: Growing, Measuring and Succeeding* (Toronto: PricewaterhouseCoopers Canada, 2006).

10. Yvan Guillemette and William B.P. Robson, "No Elixir of Youth: Immigration Cannot Keep Canada Young," *C.D. Howe Institute Backgrounder,* no. 96 (2006): 1.

11. Ibid., 8–9.

12. Statistics Canada, *Aging Well: Time Use Patterns of Older Canadians* (Ottawa: Statistics Canada, 2005).

13. Social and Economic Dimensions of an Aging Population, Projections of the Population and Labour Force to 2046: Canada, Research Paper No. 15 (McMaster University: SEDAP, 2000).

14. The Conference Board of Canada, *The Strategic Value of People, Human Resource Trends and Metrics,* Publication 003-07 (Ottawa: Conference Board of Canada, 2006), 5–17.

15. Sharon Begley, "The Upside of Aging," *The Wall Street Journal,* February 16, 2007, W1.

16. Yvan Guillemette and William B.P. Robson, "No Elixir of Youth: Immigration Cannot Keep Canada Young," *C.D. Howe Institute Backgrounder,* no. 96 (2006).

17. Paul Hodge, *Living Younger Longer: Baby Boomer Challenges,* Testimony at the White House Conference on Aging (December 11–14, 2005).

Chapter 5: The Aging Population—What It Means to You

1. United Nations Population Division, *World Population Prospects: The 2004 Revision, Medium Variant* (New York: UN Department of Economic and Social Affairs, 2005).

2. Canada Pension Plan Investment Board, *Quarterly Consolidated Financial Statements as of June 30, 2006* (Toronto: August 11, 2006).

3. Office of the Superintendent of Financial Institutions Canada, *Actuarial Report on the Canada Pension Plan as at 31 December 2003* (Ottawa: November 18, 2004).

4. Office of the Superintendent of Financial Institutions Canada, *Actuarial Report Supplementing the Actuarial Report on the Canada Pension Plan as at 31 December 2003* (Ottawa: November 28, 2006).

5. Social Security and Medicare Boards of Trustees, *Status of the Social Security and Medicare Programs: A Summary of the 2007 Annual Reports* (Washington, D.C.: U.S. Social Security Administration, 2006).

6. Jeremy J. Siegel, "Gray World," *The Wall Street Journal,* September 20, 2006, A26.

7. "Senator to Propose Raising Retirement Age," *USA Today,* July 3, 2005, www.usatoday.com/news/washington/2005-03-07-hagel-retirement_x.htm (July 3, 2005).

8. Joellen Perry, "Sweden's Pension Antidote Finds a Global Audience," *The Wall Street Journal,* March 5, 2007, A6.

9. Ben S. Bernanke, "The Coming Demographic Transition: Will We Treat Future Generations Fairly?" (speech presented to the Washington Economic Club, Washington, D.C., October 4, 2006).

10. Congressional Budget Office, *Updated Long-Term Projections for Social Security* (Washington, D.C.: Government Printing Office, June 2006).

11. Paul Hodge, "Living Younger Longer: Baby Boomer Challenges," 2005 White House Conference on Aging, December 11–14, 2005, www.genpolicy.com/articles/2005_WHCoA_Policy_Committee.html (November 8, 2006).

12. Jane Zhang and Vanessa Fuhrmans, "Government Pays Growing Share of Health Costs," *The Wall Street Journal,* February 21, 2007, A1.

13. William B.P. Robson, "Time and Money: Tracking the Fiscal Impact of Demographic Change in Canada," C.D. Howe Institute e-brief, October 5, 2006, www.cdhowe.org/pdf/ebrief_35.pdf (October 5, 2006).

Chapter 6: Lifestyle and Health Planning

1. Asset accumulation is exponential, but it is shown as linear on the graph for easier viewing. During the transition period, employment earnings are spent, but interest on savings continues to accumulate (shown as flat on the graph).

2. Lydia Saad, "Most Workers Are Positive, but One-Third Love Their Jobs," *The Gallup Poll,* August 25, 2005.

3. Joseph Carroll, "Retirement Funding Sources Differ for Current, Future Retirees," *The Gallup Poll,* June 26, 2006.

4. One particularly good source is Todd Bermont, *Career Transition Workshop: Your Complete Guide to Discovering the Ideal Job,* 2nd edition (10 Step Corporation, 2004), ISBN: 097459881-X.

5. Jeffrey M. Jones, "Only Half of Non-Retirees Expect to Be Comfortable in Retirement: Lowest Percentage in the Last Five Years," *The Gallup Poll,* May 1, 2006.

6. Lydia Saad, "Future 'Retirees' Planning to Keep Busy on the Job: Most Think They Would Still Enjoy Working," *The Gallup Poll,* June 27, 2006.

Chapter 7: Dollars and Sense

1. BMO Financial Group/Ipsos Reid, *BMO Retirement Trends Study: Presentation to BMO* (Toronto: 2005).

2. Michael Santoli, "Rich America, Poor America," *Barron's,* January 22, 2007, 21.

3. Annamaria Lusardi and Olivia S. Mitchell, "Baby Boomer Retirement Security: The Roles of Planning, Financial Literacy and Housing Wealth," Michigan Retirement Research Center, Working Paper #2006-114 (2006).

4. Capgemini Global Financial Services and Merrill Lynch & Co. Inc., *World Wealth Report: 10th Anniversary, 1997–2006* (New York: March 2006), www.ml.com/media/67216.pdf (February 16, 2006).

5. Economic Policy Institute, *State of Working America 2006/2007* (Ithaca: Cornell University Press, 2006), 247–77.

6. Government Accountability Office, *Baby Boom Generation: Retirement of Baby Boomers Is Unlikely to Precipitate Dramatic Decline in Market Returns, but Broader Risks Threaten Retirement Security* (Washington, D.C.: July 2006).

7. Ibid., 17.

8. John Gist and Carlos Figueiredo, "In Their Dreams: What Will Boomers Inherit?" AARP Public Policy Institute Research Report (2006).

9. The Strategic Counsel, *State of the Baby Boomers: A Report to BMO Financial Group* (Toronto: 2006).

10. Rachel Breitman and Del Jones, "Should Kids Be Left Fortunes or Be Left Out?" *USA Today*, July 26, 2006, 1B.

11. Matthew Miller and Tatiana Serafin, "America's 400 Richest," *Forbes* magazine, September 21, 2006, www.forbes.com/lists/2006/09/21/americas-400-richest-biz_cx_mm_06rich400_0921richintro.html (March 19, 2007).

12. Statistics Canada, Cornerstones of Community: Highlights of the National Survey of Nonprofit and Voluntary Organizations, 2003 revised (Ottawa: Statistics Canada, 2004), www.nonprofitscan.ca/pdf/NSNVO_Report_English.pdf (February 6, 2007).

Chapter 8: Have Boomers Saved Enough for Retirement?

1. Statistics Canada, *Pension Plans in Canada: Overview of Pension Plans in Canada as of January 1, 2003,* Cat. no. 13F0026MIE (Ottawa: Statistics Canada, 2004), 6–12.

2. Watson Wyatt Worldwide and the Conference Board of Canada, *Survey on Pension Plan Risk* (Ottawa: Conference Board of Canada, May 2, 2006).

3. Lucie Charron, *Canada's Pension Predicament: The Widening Gap Between Public and Private Sector Retirement Trends and Pension Plans* (Toronto: CFIB Research, January 2007).

4. Dennis Cauchon, "Pension Gap Divides Public and Private Workers," *USA Today,* February 21, 2007, 1A.

5. U.S. Bureau of Labor Statistics, *National Compensation Survey: Employee Benefits in Private Industry in the United States, March 2006* (Washington, D.C.: Government Printing Office, August 2006), 10–12, www.bls.gov/ncs/ebs/sp/ebsm0004.pdf (February 21, 2007).

6. Dennis Cauchon, "Pension Gap Divides Public and Private Workers," *USA Today,* February 21, 2007, 1A.

7. Watson Wyatt Worldwide, "The Changing Nature of Defined Benefit Plans," *Watson Wyatt Insider* 15, no. 2 (2005): 19–24.

8. M.A. Milevsky, "Spending Your Retirement in Monte Carlo," *Journal of Retirement Planning* (2001): 21–29.

9. According to the CRA, the maximum RRSP deduction limit for 2006 is $18,000. However, if you did not use your entire RRSP deduction limit for the years 1991 to 2005, you can carry forward the unused amount to 2006. Therefore, your RRSP deduction limit for 2006 may be more than $18,000. www.cra-arc.gc.ca/tax/individuals/topics/rrsp/contributing/limits-e.html (February 20, 2007).

10. Employees who are 50 years old or older at any time during the year are now allowed additional pre-tax "catch up" contributions of up to $5,000 for 2006 and 2007. The limit for future "catch up" contributions will also be adjusted for inflation in increments of $500.

11. To help ensure that companies extend their 401(k) plans to low-paid employees, an IRS rule limits the maximum deferral by the company's "highly compensated" employees, based on the average deferral by the company's non-highly compensated employees. If the rank and file save more for retirement, then the executives are allowed to save more for retirement. The calculation is rather complicated. This provision is enforced by means of "non-discrimination testing." Non-discrimination testing takes the deferral rates of "highly compensated employees" (HCEs) and compares them to non-highly compensated employees (NHCEs). An HCE is defined as an employee with compensation of $100,000 or greater in 2006 and 2007. The average deferral percentage (ADP) of all HCEs, as a group, can be no more than 2 percent greater than or 150 percent of, whichever is less, that of the NHCEs, as a group.

12. Albert B. Crenshaw and Amy Joyce, "IBM Adds Its Name to List of Firms Freezing Pensions," *The Washington Post,* January 6, 2006, A1.

13. Certified General Accountants Association of Canada, *The State of Defined Benefit Pension Plans in Canada: An Update* (Toronto: CGA, 2005).

14. The estimate, by Towers Perrin, a Stamford, Connecticut, benefits consultant, was reported in Theo Francis, "Pension Plans Take Healthy Turn: Rising Markets Aid Big Firms' Funds, Failure Risk Lessens," *The Wall Street Journal,* January 23, 2007, A4.

15. Watson Wyatt Worldwide, "More Fortune 1000 Plan Sponsors Freezing Their Defined Benefit Plans," *Watson Wyatt Insider* 16, no. 7 (2006): 2–5.

16. Alicia H. Munnell, Anthony Webb, and Luke Delorme, "A New National Retirement Risk Index," *Center for Retirement Research at Boston College, Issues in Brief* 46 (2006).

17. AXA Retirement Scope, *Retirement: A New Life after Work?* Wave 2, Canadian Results with International Comparisons (Canada: AXA, 2006).

18. Statistics Canada, *The Assets and Debts of Canadians: Focus on Private Pension Savings,* Cat. no. 13-596-XIE (Ottawa: Statistics Canada, 2001).

19. OECD, *Pensions at a Glance: Public Policies across OECD Countries* (Paris: OECD Publishing, 2005).

20. Congressional Budget Office, *The Budget and Economic Outlook: Fiscal Years 2005 to 2014* (Washington, D.C.: Congressional Budget Office, 2004).

21. William P. Bengen, *Conserving Client Portfolios During Retirement* (Denver: FPA Press, 2006), 7–15.

22. Burton Malkiel, *A Random Walk Down Wall Street* (New York: W.W. Norton, 1996).

23. Christopher Farrell, "It's All in the Timing: Sure, You Could Score Big by Riding the Market's Trends, but Even the Pros Fail To Do It Regularly," *Business Week,* February 19, 2007, 80–81.

Chapter 9: How Much Is Enough? Nest Egg Arithmetic

1. William P. Bengen, *Conserving Client Portfolios During Retirement* (Denver: FPA Press, 2006), 54.

2. There are alternative withdrawal schemes whereby people take more money in the early years of retirement when they are more

active, but they would have to take correspondingly less in the less active retirement years. This can be tough if expensive home care is needed in your later years and you are without long-term-care insurance. Many people with medical pre-conditions cannot qualify for this insurance or find it prohibitively expensive.

One of the most interesting observations from the Bengen work is that major bear markets do not derail portfolio longevity as long as you withdraw at the safe peak withdrawal rate. Bengen examined the three major bear markets over the nearly 50-year period from 1926 to 1974—1929 to 1933, 1936 to 1938, and 1973 to 1975—and found that even for people who retired at the beginning of each of these bear markets, their inflation-adjusted withdrawal rates maintained the 30-year longevity of their portfolio. The same will likely be true for those who retired at the beginning of the 2000–2002 bear market, as the bear market recoveries are usually very powerful and the bonds in a portfolio help to offset the falling value of the stocks. Also, the stock recommendations here are for large-cap companies to represent double the proportion of small-cap. Even this degree of diversification is likely enough to skate these portfolios back on side. Greater diversification into such assets as Real Estate Investment Trusts (REITs), Treasury bills, and short-term bonds, commodity futures, and others could well further improve results, but the historical data are not available to prove that point.

3. William P. Bengen, *Conserving Client Portfolios During Retirement* (Denver: FPA Press, 2006), 122.

4. M.A. Milevsky, "Spending Your Retirement in Monte Carlo," *Journal of Retirement Planning,* (2001): 21–29.

5. David Nawrocki, "Problems with Monte Carlo Simulation," *Journal of Financial Planning* (November 2001).

6. The 401(k) plan in the United States may be more generous than an RRSP.

The non-partisan Employee Benefit Research Institute estimates that there are 12.1 million people in the United States eligible for workplace retirement plans who don't participate. The Pension Protection Act of 2006 now allows automatic enrolment. Employees can opt out of the plan, but they are more likely to stay put out of inertia. To address the problem that people do not save enough for retirement, the new law makes it easier for companies to automatically increase the percentage of an employee's salary that is directed to the plan.

The new rules don't increase the amount of money an individual can put into a 401(k), but they do encourage companies to meet certain minimum step-ups going from a 3 percent employee contribution the first year to 4 percent the second year and up to 6 percent the fourth year. Also, companies are encouraged to meet certain minimum requirements when matching the automatic deductions with additional employer contributions.

The federal limit on annual contributions to a 401(k) has risen gradually to a maximum employee contribution of $15,500 in 2007 (or $20,500 if you are age 50 and older; the additional $5,000 is your "catch-up" contribution), below the $19,000 RRSP limit that year. These are the IRS limits, but you are also subject to the limits imposed by your company's 401(k) plan. Moreover, employer matching contributions are not counted as part of this contribution limit, as they are in Canada. As I discussed earlier, the maximum annual combined 401(k) contribution is the lesser of 100 percent of income or $45,000, although very few Americans get that much, because it would require nearly two-to-one matching of $30,000 by the employer, far more generous than most actual 401(k) plans. The typical match is 50 cents on the dollar up to 6 percent of your salary.

7. The examples assume annual income growth of 2.5 percent.

8. Michael K. Stein, *The Prosperous Retirement* (Boulder: Emptsco LLC, 1998).

9. Some insurance companies are offering annuities that begin paying 20 years after the purchase date, which is considerably less expensive, because they get the compound return on your money over that period. Of course, you forfeit the money if you die before payout begins.

Chapter 10: Health and Happiness in Act III

1. George E. Vaillant, *Adaptation to Life* (Boston: First Harvard University Press, 1995).

2. Michael F. Roizen, *Real Age: Are You as Young as You Can Be?* (New York: HarperCollins, 1999).

3. William J. Cromie, "How to Be Happy and Well Rather Than Sad and Sick," *Harvard University Gazette*, June 7, 2001, www.news.harvard.edu/gazette/2001/06.07/01-happywell.html (February 27, 2007).

4. George E. Vaillant, *Adaptation to Life* (Boston: First Harvard University Press, 1995), 75–90.

5. George E. Vaillant, *Aging Well* (New York: Little, Brown and Company, 2001).

6. George E. Vaillant, "Mental Health," *American Journal of Psychiatry* 160 (August 2003): 1377, http://ajp.psychiatryonline.org/cgi/reprint/160/8/1373.pdf (March 4, 2007).

7. Ibid., 1377.

8. K. Warner Schaie, "The Seattle Longitudinal Study: A 21-Year Exploration of Psychometric Intelligence in Adulthood," *Longitudinal Studies of Adult Psychological Development* (1983): 64–135.

9. P.I. Yakovlev and A.R. Lecours, "The Myelogenetic Cycles of Regional Maturation of the Brain," *Regional Development of the Brain in Early Life,* edited by A. Minkowski (1967): 3–69.

10. George E. Vaillant, *Aging Well* (New York: Little, Brown and Company, 2001).

11. E.H. Erikson, "Growth and Crises of the Healthy Personality," in *Symposium on the Healthy Personality: Supplement II of the Fourth Conference on Infancy and Childhood,* edited by M. Senn (1950): 1–95.

12. George E. Vaillant, "Mental Health," *American Journal of Psychiatry* 160 (2003): 1378, http://ajp.psychiatryonline.org/cgi/reprint/160/8/1373.pdf (March 4, 2007).

13. Gail Sheehy, *Passages: Predictable Crises of Adult Life* (New York: E.P. Dutton, 1976).

Bibliography

Abelson, Alan. "The Medicare Scam." *Barron's* (August 28, 2006), www.barrons.com (August 28, 2006).

AXA Retirement Scope. *Retirement: A New Life After Work?* Wave 2, Canadian Results with International Comparisons. Canada: AXA, 2006.

Begley, Sharon. "The Upside of Aging." *The Wall Street Journal* (February 16, 2007): W1.

Bengen, William P. *Conserving Client Portfolios During Retirement.* Denver: FPA Press, 2006.

Bermont, Todd. *Career Transition Workshop: Your Complete Guide to Discovering the Ideal Job,* 2nd edition. 10 Step Corporation, 2004.

Bernanke, Ben S. "The Coming Demographic Transition: Will We Treat Future Generations Fairly?" Speech presented to the Washington Economic Club, Washington D.C., October 4, 2006.

BMO Financial Group/Ipsos Reid. *BMO Retirement Trends Study.* Toronto: BMO Financial Group, 2005.

Bradsher, Keith. "The Next Industrial Giant Is ... India?" *The New York Times* (August 31, 2006), www.nytimes.com/2006/08/31/business/31cnd-rupee.html?ex=1314676800&en=3d19abd279037e05&ei=5088&partner=rssnyt&emc=rss (August 31, 2006).

Breitman, Rachel, and Del Jones. "Should Kids Be Left Fortunes, Or Be Left Out?" *USA Today* (July 26, 2006): 1B.

Bureau of Labor Statistics (U.S.). *Monthly Labor Review.* Washington, D.C.: Bureau of Labor Statistics, 2007.

———. *National Compensation Survey: Employee Benefits in Private Industry in the United States, March 2006.* Washington, D.C.: Bureau of Labor Statistics, 2006.

Butler, Robert N. *Why Survive: Being Old in America.* New York: Harper & Row, 1975.

Canada Pension Plan Investment Board. *Quarterly Consolidated Financial Statements as of June 30, 2006.* Toronto: CPP Investment Board, 2006.

Capgemini Global Financial Services and Merrill Lynch & Co. *World Wealth Report: 10th Anniversary, 1997–2006.* New York: Merrill Lynch, 2006.

Carlson, Robert C. *The New Rules of Retirement: Strategies for a Secure Future.* New Jersey: John Wiley & Sons, 2005.

Carroll, Joseph. "Pension Gap Divides Public and Private Workers." *USA Today* (February 21, 2007).

Cauchon, Dennis. "Focusing on the Issue of Aging, and Growing into the Job." *The New York Times* (November 14, 2006): S2.

———. "Pension Gap Divides Public and Private Workers." *USA Today* (February 21, 2007).

Center on Budget and Policy Priorities. *The Number of Uninsured Americans Is at an All-Time High.* Washington, D.C.: Center on Budget and Policy Priorities, 2006: 1.

Certified General Accountants Association of Canada. *The State of Defined Benefit Pension Plans in Canada: An Update.* Toronto: CGA, 2005.

Charron, Lucie. *Canada's Pension Predicament: The Widening Gap Between Public and Private Sector Retirement Trends and Pension Plans.* Toronto: Canadian Federation of Independent Business, Research Report, January 2007.

Collins, Jim. *Good to Great.* New York: HarperCollins, 2001.

Conference Board of Canada. *The Strategic Value of People, Human Resource Trends and Metrics,* Publication 003-07. Ottawa: The Conference Board of Canada, 2006: 5–17.

Congressional Budget Office. *The Budget and Economic Outlook: Fiscal Years 2005 to 2014.* A Report to the Senate and House Committees on the Budget. Washington, D.C.: Government Printing Office, 2004.

———. *Updated Long-Term Projections for Social Security.* Washington, D.C.: Government Printing Office, 2006.

Cooper, Sherry. *The Cooper Files.* Toronto: Key Porter, 1999.

———. *Ride the Wave.* Toronto: Financial Times Prentice Hall Canada, 2001.

Crenshaw, Albert B., and Amy Joyce. "IBM Adds Its Name to List of Firms Freezing Pensions." *The Washington Post* (January 6, 2006): A01.

Cromie, William J. "How To Be Happy and Well Rather Than Sad and Sick." *Harvard University Gazette* (June 7, 2001), www.news.harvard.edu/gazette/2001/06.07/01-happywell.html (February 27, 2007).

Di Mento, Maria, and Nicole Lewis. "Record-Breaking Giving: More Than 20 Americans Contributed at Least $100 million to Charity Last Year, a Chronicle Survey Finds." *The Chronicle of Philanthropy, Gifts & Grants* (February 22, 2007), www.philantrhopy.com/free/articles/v19/i09/09000601.htm (February 27, 2007).

Dreifus, Claudia. "Focusing on the Issue of Aging, and Growing into the Job." *The New York Times* (November 14, 2006): S2.

Dychtwald, Ken, Tamara J. Erickson, and Robert Morison. *Workforce Crisis: How to Beat the Coming Shortage of Skills and Talent.* Boston: Harvard Business School Press, 2006.

Economic Policy Institute. *State of Working America 2006/2007.* Ithaca: Cornell University Press, 2006: 247–77.

Eisenberg, Lee. *The Number.* New York: Free Press, 2006.

Erikson, E.H. "Growth and Crises of the Healthy Personality." *Symposium on the Healthy Personality: Supplement II of the Fourth Conference on Infancy and Childhood,* edited by M. Senn (1950): 1–95.

Farrell, Christopher. "It's All in the Timing: Sure, You Could Score Big by Riding the Market's Trends—But Even the Pros Fail to Do It Regularly." *Business Week* (February 19, 2007): 80–81.

Fein, Esther B. "Book Notes." *The New York Times* (November 20, 1991), query.nytimes.com/gst/fullpage.html?sec=health&res=9D0 CE7D61339F933A15752C1A967958260 (November 28, 2006).

Felder, Stefan. "The Gender Longevity Gap: Explaining the Difference between Singles and Couples." *Journal of Population Economics,* 19, no. 3 (2006): 543–57.

Feng, Chen. "China Has Not Relaxed Family Planning: Official." *China View: Xinhua online* (in English) (May 1, 2006), news.xinhuanet.com/english/2006-05/01/content_4499663.htm (February 15, 2006).

———. "Official Calls for Criminalization of Sex Identification." *China View: Xinhua online* (in English) (1 May 2006), news.xinhuanet.com/english/2006-05/01/content_4499663.htm (15 February 2006).

Frankl, Victor E. *Man's Search for Meaning.* New York: Perseus Publishing, 2000.

Gist, John, and Carlos Figueiredo. "In Their Dreams: What Will Boomers Inherit?" AARP Public Policy Institute Research Report (2006).

Government Accountability Office. *Baby Boom Generation: Retirement of Baby Boomers Is Unlikely to Precipitate Dramatic Decline in Market Returns, but Broader Risks Threaten Retirement Security.* Washington, D.C.: Government Accountability Office, 2006.

Guillemette, Yvan, and William B.P. Robson. "No Elixir of Youth: Immigration Cannot Keep Canada Young." *C.D. Howe Institute Backrounder,* no. 96 (2006).

Hodge, Paul. "Living Younger Longer: Baby Boomer Challenges." Testimony at the White House Conference on Aging (December 11–14, 2005).

Hudson, Valerie M., and Andrea M. Den Boer. *Bare Branches: The Security Implications of Asia's Surplus Male Population.* Boston: MIT Press, 2004.

Ibbotson Associates Inc. *Stocks, Bonds, Bills and Inflation: 2005 Yearbook.* Chicago: Ibbotson Associates Inc., 2005.

James, Phillip T., Rachel Leach, Eleni Kalamara, and Maryam Shayeghi. "Obesity, the Major Health Issue of the 21st Century: The Worldwide Obesity Epidemic." *The North American Association for the Study of Obesity* (2001), www.obesityresearch.org/cgi/content/full/9/suppl_4/S228#F1 (February 19, 2006).

Jones, Jeffrey M. "Only Half of Non-Retirees Expect to Be Comfortable in Retirement: Lowest Percentage in the Last Five Years." *The Gallup Poll* (May 1, 2006).

Kessler, Andy. *The End of Medicine: How Silicon Valley (and Naked Mice) Will Reboot Your Doctor.* New York: HarperCollins, 2006.

Klein, Dr. Samuel. Email interview by Dr. Sherry Cooper. Toronto, February 19, 2007.

Kolata, Gina. "So Big and Healthy, Grandpa Wouldn't Even Know You." *The New York Times* (July 30, 2006), www.nytimes.com/2006/07/30/health/30age.html?ei=5070&en=55ee76d6029951f5&ex=1172293200&adxnnl=1&adxnnlx=1172166163-wWmk GIoc4KWOrf8BYGZQMw (July 30, 2006).

Kostigen, Thomas. "Like Your Own Foundation: Popularity of Donor-Advised Funds Grows." *Dow Jones Market Watch, Sophisticated Investor* (November 9, 2006), www.marketwatch.com/

News/Story/Story.aspx?dist=newsfinder&siteid=mktw&guid=%7
B2B6C0DA3%2D74ED%2D41D9%2D81D8%2DF252047A4
E5C%7D&link=&keyword=Thomas%20Kostigen&print=true&
dist=printTop (February 6, 2007).

Kotlikoff, Laurence J., and Scott Burns. *The Coming Generational Storm: What You Need to Know about America's Economic Future.* Boston: MIT Press, 2005.

Kuller, Dr. Lewis H. Email interview by Dr. Sherry Cooper. Toronto, February 15, 2007.

Landler, Mark. "McCain, in Vietnam, Finds the Past Isn't Really Past." *The New York Times* (April 27, 2000), query.nytimes.com/gst/full page.html?res=9F07E3D91130F934A15757C0A9669C8B63 (April 27, 2000).

Lipschitz, Dr. David. "About Dr. David." Dr. David Health.com, Breaking the Rules of Aging (2007), www.drdavidhealth.com/section.asp?secID=10 (December 10, 2006).

Lovett-Reid, Patricia. *Live Well Retire Well.* Toronto: TD Waterhouse Canada, 2006.

Lusardi, Annamaria, and Olivia S. Mitchell. "Baby Boomer Retirement Security: The Roles of Planning, Financial Literacy and Housing Wealth." Michigan Retirement Research Center, Working Paper 2006-114 (2006).

Malkeil, Burton. *A Random Walk Down Wall Street.* New York: W.W. Norton & Company, 1996.

Mandel, Michael, and Joseph Weber. "What's Really Propping Up the Economy: Since 2001, the Health-Care Industry Has Added 1.7 Million Jobs. The Rest of the Private Sector?" *BusinessWeek Online* (September 25, 2006), www.businessweek.com/magazine/content/06_39/b4002001.thm (February 6, 2007).

Marrero, D.G. "Time to Get Moving: Helping Patients with Diabetes Adopt Exercise as Part of a Healthy Lifestyle." *Clinical Diabetes,* 23, 4 (2005): 154–59.

Merman, Gordon B.T., Richard W. Johnson, and Dan Murphy. "Why Do Boomers Plan to Work So Long?" The Urban Institute, Discussion Paper 06-04 (2006): 12.

Milevsky, M.A., and Anna Abaimova. "Retirement Ruin and the Sequencing of Returns." The IFID Centre (2006).

———. "Spending Your Retirement in Monte Carlo." *Journal of Retirement Planning* (2001): 21–29.

Milken Institute. "Global Conference: Expanding Opportunities in the Global Marketplace, Speaker's List." Conference Links, milkeninstitute.org/events/gcprogram.taf?function=speakers&even tid=gc06 (February 13, 2007).

Miller, Lee E., and Jessica Miller. *A Woman's Guide to Successful Negotiating*. New York: McGraw-Hill, 2002.

Miller, Matthew, and Tatiana Serafin. "America's 400 Richest." *Forbes* magazine (September 21, 2006).

Mintz, Jack M. "The 2006 Competitiveness Report: Proposals for Pro-Growth Tax Reform." *C.D. Howe Institute Commentary*, 239, (2006).

Munnell, Alicia H., Anthony Webb, and Luke Delorme. "A New National Retirement Risk Index." *Center for Retirement Research at Boston College, Issues in Brief*, 46 (2006).

NAASO: The Obesity Society. "Medical Complications of Obesity." www.obesityonline.org/slides (October 10, 2006).

Nash, Laura, and Howard Stevenson. *Just Enough: Tools for Creating Success in Your Work and Life*. New Jersey: John Wiley & Sons, 2004.

Nawrocki, David. "Problems with Monte Carlo Simulation." *Journal of Financial Planning*, 12, (2001).

OECD. *Pensions at a Glance: Public Policies across OECD Countries*. Paris: OECD Publishing, 2005.

Office of the Superintendent of Financial Institutions Canada. *Actuarial Report on the Canada Pension Plan as at the 31st of December 2003*. Ottawa: 2004.

———. *Actuarial Report Supplementing the Actuarial Report on the Canada Pension Plan as at the 31st of December 2003*. Ottawa: 2006.

Ontario Ministry of Labour. *Pregnancy Leave and Parental Leave*. Toronto: Ontario Ministry of Labour, 2006.

Pape, Gordon. *The Retirement Time Bomb: How to Achieve Financial Independence in a Changing World*. Toronto: Penguin Canada, 2006.

Perry, Joellen. "Sweden's Pension Antidote Finds a Global Audience." *The Wall Street Journal* (March 5, 2007), online.wsj.com/article/SB117306202234226586.html (March 6, 2007).

PriceWaterhouseCoopers. *The 2006 Survey of Canadian Private Companies: Growing, Measuring and Succeeding*. Toronto: PriceWaterhouseCoopers Canada, 2006.

Rabin, Roni. "Health Disparities Persist for Men, and Doctors Ask Why." *The New York Times* (November 14, 2006), www.nytimes.com/2006/11/14/health/14men.html?ex=13211604 00&en=1668bbac347e8d5d&ei=5088&partner=rssnyt&emc=rss (November 14, 2006).

Roberts, Sam. "51% of Women Are Now Living Without Spouse." *The New York Times* (January 16, 2007): A1.

Robson, William B.P. "Time and Money: Tracking the Fiscal Impact of Demographic Change in Canada." *C.D. Howe Institute e-brief* (October 5, 2006), www.cdhowe.org/pdf/ebrief_35.pdf (October 5, 2006).

Roizen, Michael F. *Real Age: Are You as Young as You Can Be?* New York: HarperCollins, 1999.

Saad, Lydia. "Future 'Retirees' Planning to Keep Busy on the Job: Most Think They Would Still Enjoy Working." *The Gallup Poll* (June 27, 2006).

———. "Most Workers Are Positive, but One-Third Love Their Jobs." *The Gallup Poll* (August 25, 2005).

Sabelhaas, John, and Joyce Manchester. "Baby Boomers and Their Parents: How Does Their Economic Well-Being Compare in Middle Age?" *The Journal of Human Resources,* 30, no. 4 (1995): 791–806.

Santoli, Michael. "Rich America, Poor America." *Barron's* (January 22, 2007): 21.

Savage, Terry. *The Savage Number.* New Jersey: John Wiley & Sons, 2005.

Schaie, K. Warner. "The Seattle Longitudinal Study: A 21-Year Exploration of Psychometric Intelligence in Adulthood." *Longitudinal Studies of Adult Psychological Development.* New York: Guilford, 1983.

Schulz, James H. *The Economics of Aging,* 7th edition. Connecticut: Auburn House Paperback, 2000.

"Senator to Propose Raising Retirement Age." *USA Today* (July 3, 2005), www.usatoday.com/news/washington/2005-03-07-hagel-retirement_x.htm (March 26, 2007).

Sheehy, Gail. *Passages: Predictable Crises of Adult Life.* New York: E.P. Dutton, 1976.

Shellenbarger, Sue. "More New Mothers Are Staying Home Even When It Causes Financial Pain." *The Wall Street Journal* (November 30, 2006): D1.

Siegel, Jeremy J. "Gray World." *The Wall Street Journal* (September 20, 2006): A26.

Social Security and Medicare Boards of Trustees. *Status of the Social Security and Medicare Programs: A Summary of the 2006 Annual Reports.* Washington, D.C.: U.S. Social Security Administration, 2006.

Social and Economic Dimensions of an Aging Population, Projections of the Population and Labour Force to 2046: Canada, Research Paper No. 15 (McMaster University: SEDAP, 2000).

Stannard-Stockton, Sean. "Baby Boomers Changing Philanthropy." *Tactical Philanthropy* (October 19, 2006), www.tacticalphilan thropy.com/2006/10/baby_boomers_ch.html (February 6, 2007).

Statistics Canada. *Aging Well: Time Use Patterns of Older Canadians.* Ottawa: Statistics Canada, 2006.

———. *The Assets and Debts of Canadians: Focus on Private Pension Savings,* Cat. no. 13-596-XIE. Ottawa: Statistics Canada, 2001.

———. *Cornerstones of Community: Highlights of the National Survey of Nonprofit and Voluntary Organizations.* Ottawa: Statistics Canada, 2004.

———. *The Daily: General Social Survey—Social Support and Ageing,* Cat. no. 11-001-XIE. Ottawa: Statistics Canada, 2003: 2–3.

———. *Pension Plans in Canada: Overview of Data on Pension Plans in Canada as of January 1, 2003,* Cat. no. 13f-0026-MIE. Ottawa: Statistics Canada, 2003: 6–20.

Stein, Michael K. *The Prosperous Retirement.* Boulder: Emptsco LLC, 1998.

Strategic Counsel. *State of the Baby Boomers—A Report to BMO Financial Group.* Toronto: The Strategic Counsel, 2006.

Sullivan, P.W., E.H. Morrato, V. Ghushchyan, H.R. Wyatt, and J.O. Hill. "Obesity, Inactivity, and the Prevalence of Diabetes and Diabetes-Related Cardiovascular Comorbidities in the U.S., 2000–2002." *Diabetes Care,* 28, 7 (2006): 1599–1603.

Theo, Francis. "Pension Plans Take Healthy Turn: Rising Markets Aid Big Firms' Funds; Failure Risk Lessens." *The Wall Street Journal* (January 23, 2007): A4.

United Nations Population Division. *World Population Prospects: The 2004 Revision—Medium Variant.* New York: UN Department of Economic and Social Affairs, 2005.

Vaillant, George E. *Adaptation to Life.* Boston: Harvard University Press, 1995.

———. *Aging Well.* New York: Little, Brown and Company, 2001.

———. "Mental Health." *American Journal of Psychiatry,* 160 (2003): 1377.

Watson Wyatt Insider. *The Changing Nature of Defined Benefit Plans.* Watson Wyatt Worldwide, 2005.

———. *More Fortune 1000 Plan Sponsors Freezing Their Defined Benefit Plans.* Watson Wyatt Worldwide, 2006.

Watson Wyatt Worldwide and the Conference Board of Canada. *Survey on Pension Plan Risk.* Ottawa: Conference Board of Canada, 2006.

"The Wellness Boom." *The Economist* (January 6, 2007): 51.

Wiseman, Paul. "China Thrown off Balance As Boys Outnumber Girls." *USA Today* (June 19, 2002), www.usatoday.com/news/world/2002/06/19/china-usat.htm (February 15, 2007).

Woodard, Dustin. "What Are the 2007 401(k) Contribution Limits?" About.com: Mutual Funds (February 20, 2007), mutualfunds.about.com/od/retirement/a/2007_limits.htm (February 20, 2007).

World Health Organization. *Preventing Chronic Diseases: A Vital Investment,* ISBN: 92-4-156300-1. Geneva: World Health Organization, 2005: 74–83.

Yakovlev, P.I., and A.R. Lecour. *The Myelogenetic Cycles of Regional Maturation of the Brain: Regional Development of the Brain in Early Life.* Oxford: Blackwell Scientific, 1983.

Yang, Catherine, and Kerry Capell. "Another Case Entirely: The Former AOL Chairman's Last Gig: A Daring Bet on Hospitality and Health Care." *BusinessWeek* (April 11, 2005), www.businessweek.com/magazine/content/05_15/b3928093.htm (December 13, 2006).

Zelinski, Ernie J. *How to Retire Happy, Wild, and Free.* Berkeley: Ten Speed Press, 2007.

Zhang, Jane, and Vanessa Fuhrmans. "Government Pays Growing Share of Health Costs." *The Wall Street Journal* (February 21, 2007): A1.

Acknowledgments

I would like to thank Andrea Magyar, editorial director at Penguin Group (Canada), for her confidence, support, and invaluable advice on yet another book. Andrea, it is always a pleasure to work with you and know that my project is in good hands. My editor, Alexander Schultz, enhanced my prose and asked all of the right questions. Alex, it is great that you could spot the economics jargon and replace it with real English, making this book far more readable and accessible even to the financial-phobes among us.

The Private Client Group at BMO Bank of Montreal provided the impetus for this project by asking me to present at retirement/regeneration seminars across Canada beginning in the spring of 2006. BMO is committed to providing unparalleled retirement and financial-planning services and has come to know the needs of the pre-retiree in Canada through extensive surveys and conversations with many Canadian boomers. It was through this market research that it first became evident that boomers will be "retiring" in a new way, reinventing themselves as they proceed along a retirement path very different from that of their parents. Thinking about these issues for myself sparked my interest in delving further, as boomers' life passages continue to influence the trends of the economy and financial markets, and will continue to do so as long as we live.

Kris Vikmanis, head of the Retirement Market at BMO, has reviewed this book; our discussions regarding the new retirement have been quite helpful. I would also like to acknowledge Peter

Hanson, senior manager of Enterprise Financial Planning Programs for the Retirement Market at BMO, for reviewing parts of this work and verifying the nest egg arithmetic. Caroline Dabu, head of Private Client Group Marketing, also read a draft; thank you, Caroline, for the much-needed encouragement.

As my research progressed, I realized that the planning of what might be decades of life in retirement required more than just a financial or economic plan. My thanks go to chief medical officer Dr. Elaine Chin and naturopathic doctor Dr. Shelley Burns of Scienta Health, a clinic that provides leading-edge diagnostics and protocols for maximum wellness and is a pioneer in genomics-based individualized health management. Through them, I have come to learn and appreciate a proactive approach to health. I also want to acknowledge Dr. Gordon Tisdall for helping me to understand the psychological and somatic aspects of successful aging; I have benefited well beyond this book from his ability to provide insight on life's passages. It is through him that I learned that the full maturation of the human mind takes nearly a complete lifetime—that old dogs do learn new tricks.

Once again, my utmost appreciation and thanks to Jennifer Lee, manager and economist at BMO Capital Markets, a great colleague and dear friend. Jennifer has seen me through three books in eight years. We have worked together for well over a decade and I have come to rely on her impeccable economic assistance. Thank you, as well, to Robert Kavcic, who provided excellent research and technical support. For a while there, Robert was answering questions on weekends about the minutia of government and business pension plans. Robert is likely one of the best-prepared 20-somethings for retirement 40 years hence. Benjamin Reitzes, another economist at BMO Capital Markets, also provided reliable research assistance. Daniel Jankowski provided virtually round-the-clock expert technical and research assistance. Not only is Daniel an amazing technology wizard and media designer, but he also knows quite a lot about many things. Daniel, I can't thank you enough for your patience, diligence, and instant recall.

The many aspects of my life and work require tremendous support from a few key people. Trudy Verkaik is my major-domo and takes responsibility for my calendar, which makes her the equivalent of an air-traffic controller as well. Thanks go as well to Thelma Flores and Carmen Grant for many years of loyal service.

The views expressed in this book are my own and do not necessarily represent the views of the Bank of Montreal Financial Group or any of its employees. Much of the credit goes to these many people, but any errors or omissions are my own.

Finally, but far from last, my love and thanks go to Peter Cooper, my husband and soulmate, for giving me the room to pursue my dreams, the encouragement to believe in them, and a partner to share them with. Love and gratitude as well to my mother, Vilma Sussman Liedman, and my amazing son, Stefan Atkinson; I am grateful to you both for your support and wisdom.

Index

Italicized numbers connote charts, tables, illustrations.